Rumer Godden Revisited

Twayne's English Authors Series
Children's Literature

Lois R. Kuznets, Editor
San Diego State University

TEAS 519

RUMER GODDEN
Photo by Jerry Bauer

Rumer Godden Revisited

Lynne M. Rosenthal

Mercy College, New York

Twayne Publishers
An Imprint of Simon & Schuster Macmillan
New York

Prentice Hall International
London • Mexico City • New Delhi • Singapore • Sydney • Toronto

Twayne's English Authors Series No. 519

Rumer Godden Revisited
Lynne M. Rosenthal

Twayne Publishers
An Imprint of Simon & Schuster Macmillan
1633 Broadway
New York, NY 10019

Library of Congress Cataloging-in-Publication Data

Rosenthal, Lynne Meryl.
    Rumer Godden revisited / by Lynne M. Rosenthal.
        p.   cm.— (Twayne's English authors series ; TEAS 519)
    Includes bibliographical references and index.
    ISBN 0-8057-7930-2 (cloth)
    1. Godden, Rumer, 1907–   —Criticism and interpretation.
    2. Women and literature—England—History—20th century.   3. Women
    and literature—India—History—20th century.   I. Title.
    II. Series.
PR6013.OZ87   1996
823'.912—dc20   95-43845
                                                                                    CIP
                                                                                    AC

The paper used in this publication meets the minimum requirements of American
National Standard for Information Sciences—Permanence of Paper for Printed Library
Materials, ANSI Z39.48-1984. ∞™

10 9 8 7 6 5 4 3 2 1

Printed in the United States of America.

For Helen and Sabrina
and in memory of
Sheila, Ida, and Max Schlesinger
and Alana Leslye Collos,
whose voices continue to live
in my own "house with four rooms"

—L.M.R.

Contents

Preface

In her essay "The Will to Write," Rumer Godden quotes Chekhov: "What is needed is constant work, day and night, constant reading, study, will . . . every hour is precious for it."[1] Chekhov's words may well be taken as an emblem of the literary and personal life of this much loved and prolific writer whose works for children and adults cover a span of more than five decades and include an impressive range of novels, stories, verse, criticism, biography, and autobiography.

Godden was, and remains, a natural storyteller. In the epigraph of her third autobiography, *A House with Four Rooms,* Godden asserts her identity as a teller of stories: "To me and my kind life itself is a story and we have to tell it in stories—that is the way it falls. I have told the truth and nothing but the truth, yet not the whole truth, because that would be impossible."[2]

Set in England, India, and the Scotland of her more recent years, Godden's novels reflect a variety of experiences in which self-transformation occurs through an act of will. For Godden, whether describing the worlds of upper-class Anglos and Indians or those of street children, Gypsies, nuns, prostitutes, or ballet dancers, it seems necessary to retell a story from various perspectives to attain her objective of truthful writing. In reformulating stories about the ways in which adults and children struggle to furnish all the rooms of the self (physical, mental, emotional, and spiritual, as described in *A House with Four Rooms*), Godden achieves in her work a sense of continuity and timelessness despite change.

As William York Tindall observes, Godden's best work may be seen within the "great symbolist movement of our time."[3] Images such as the house, the river, the garden, and the vastness of India itself link dimensions of time and space, attesting to continuity within change. Although religious imagery figures in a number of Godden's works, spirituality goes beyond conventional forms. Permeating Godden's writing is a faith that deeply felt wishes (which seem to serve as a form of prayer), when allied with hard work and integrity, are rewarded by the universe. In many cases, the reward extends beyond the individual and serves as a form of social grace in which others are mysteriously helped as well.

This volume is a contemporary, updated review, written a generation after Hassell Simpson completed his Twayne study in 1973 (until this volume the only existing full-length study of Godden's work). *Rumer Godden Revisited* views Godden's books for adults and children from a new perspective and, in so doing, approaches a fuller sense of the "truth" of Godden's writing. This retrospective is a timely one for several reasons.

In the years since Simpson's book appeared, Godden has added two autobiographies and numerous books for children and adults to her already extensive collection. Indeed, just as readers believe they have read everything Godden has written, to their delight a new book appears on the adult or juvenile shelf of the library. Godden's new work needs to be viewed in the context of the entirety of her oeuvre.

A second reason this review is a timely one is its focus. In his study, Simpson focused on Godden's novels for adults. Because she had published only one major novel (*In This House of Brede*) between 1963 and 1973, Simpson prophesied that her career as a novelist was probably complete. If the search for continuity is central to Godden's work, however, as this new study suggests, predictability is not. Since 1973, Godden has published four novels for adults: *Five for Sorrow; Ten for Joy: A Novel* (1979, its subtitle subtly undercutting Simpson's prediction); *The Dark Horse* (1981); *Coromandel, Sea Change* (1990); and *Pippa Passes* (1994). She has also published three full-length novels for children or young people—*The Peacock Spring* (1975), *Thursday's Children* (1984), and *Listen to the Nightingale* (1992)—in addition to shorter works for children and adults. If a shift in direction has taken place since Simpson's study, it may be more accurate to see it as one in which Godden has increasingly concentrated on writing for and addressing child audiences, publishing ten children's books and engaging in public readings of poems by authors such as Gerard Manley Hopkins and Dylan Thomas to interest children in poetry.

Central to Godden's adult and children's books is a profound concern about how children are affected by adults' choices as well as by their own, about how *wanting*—in both senses of the word, *lacking* and *wishing*—and *getting* influence a child's development. The importance of the image of the child in Godden's work should not be surprising to the reader. Godden was, for all intents and purposes, a single parent in the 1940s (and the central figure in her children's lives both when married and when unmarried). Awareness of the tension between the domestic and creative angels (or demons) is expressed throughout her work in a variety of ways, as female protagonists feel torn between home and family on the one hand, and art or love, which are often seen to lie beyond the home, on the other.

Social change and a wide range of feminist criticism have finally made it necessary to go beyond Simpson's view of the women in Godden's novels as "less than womanly" because they cannot easily resolve the conflict between domestic and creative impulses.[4] Today, the single parent (by divorce or by choice), unlike Godden in the 1940s, is no longer a rarity. Even in two-parent homes, children, for better or worse, are increasingly on their own. Godden's insights into the varieties of ways in which children respond when imperfectly parented speaks to our need to understand our children and ourselves.

The causes and repercussions of the fact that women, in literature and life, have traditionally tended to view women's choices as mutually exclusive have been explored in recent years by feminist critics. In exploring psychoanalytic object-relations theory in *The Reproduction of Mothering,* Nancy Chodorow observes that children develop a sense of self mainly in relation to the degree of empathy they perceive in the mother or primary caretaker. If, as Sara Ruddick asserts in *Maternal Thinking,* maternal holding or nurturing of the child can be contrasted with a more separate, worldly reality represented by the father, what happens when the mother's needs are at odds with the child's? Is it true, as Freud argued and Chodorow suggests, that the child's eventual recognition of the sometimes imperfect nature of mother-love creates frustration and anxiety that enable the child to grow, and that this recognition contributes to the development of a stronger and more integrated self?

How children respond when parental, mostly maternal "holding" is inadequate is a question that Godden was perhaps one of the first novelists to explore both in literature written for children and in that written for adults. How do children whose parents have placed their own needs ahead of those of their offspring fare when left on their own in any or all of the four rooms of the self described in *A House with Four Rooms?* Do they suffer irreparable damage in silent or obvious ways? Or do children discover and develop, with the aid of internal and external images and helping figures, with imagination and art, the resources that, as Godden's characters often assert, "stretch" them in unexpected ways? But if the latter, at what cost to the child? And do child characters fare differently in books written for children and for adults?

The following study is, then, focused on the image of the child and of childhood in Godden's writing for children and adults over the past five decades. Whether in Godden's animal, doll, children's, or adult stories, I here suggest that the child or adolescent, most often female, serves as a powerful mirroring image, reflecting many of society's most profound fears, struggles, and hopes for redemption. My study focuses on the seminal image of the child to achieve a more finely tuned insight into Godden's work as a whole as it explores the many strata of the life cycle.

Following a biographical chapter, this text is arranged chronologically. Juvenile and adult books are reviewed together in chronological order, in part because many of Godden's works have been shelved under either label by different libraries. *An Episode of Sparrows* (1955), for example, written for adults, is commonly found in children's libraries, while *The Kitchen Madonna* (1967) and *The Diddakoi* (1972) were published in England for children and in America for adults as well. The chronological structure of this book also best reflects the pattern of Godden's development as a writer and the evolution of recurrent themes that seem to comment on and sometimes complete one another.

Although the books that have been selected for discussion are those in which the image of the child is central, or those which were written for child readers, in some books the absence or peripheral nature of the child is also significant. Books in which the child appears marginally or not at all are, if relevant, discussed at the beginning or conclusion of appropriate chapters. Finally, the concluding chapter offers a brief review and attempts to answer some of the questions posed throughout.

Chronology

1907	Margaret Rumer Godden born 10 December in Eastbourne, Sussex, to Katherine Norah Hingley and Arthur Leigh Godden.
1908	Is taken by parents to India, where her father works in navigation. The family lives in several places on the rivers of Assam and Bengal.
1913	Sent to grandmother's London house for a year's stay.
1914	Returns to India in November because of World War I.
1920	Goes back to England for schooling. Attends five schools in five years, then trains as a ballet teacher and returns to India.
1928	Opens a dancing school for children in Calcutta.
1934	Marries Laurence Sinclair Foster in Calcutta. Father retires to first of two homes in Cornwall, Darrynane House.
1935	Birth of first daughter, Jane, in London.
1936	*Chinese Puzzle* is published.
1938	Birth of second daughter, Paula, in Cornwall. *The Lady and the Unicorn* is published.
1939	*Black Narcissus* is published. Godden takes daughters to India because of World War II.
1940	*Gypsy, Gypsy* is published.
1942	*Breakfast with the Nikolides* is published. Separates from Laurence, who remains with his army regiment in India. Godden lives nearby, having little contact with him.
1943–1944	Lives with children at Dove House in Kashmir, rent-free, then returns to England.
1945	Next novel is published in England as *A Fugue in Time* and in America as *Take Three Tenses*.
1946	*The River* is published. Godden and Laurence divorce.

1947 *The Dolls' House*, Godden's first children's book, is published. Godden moves to Arundel, Sussex.

1948 *A Candle for St. Jude* is published.

1949 Moves to Speen, Aylesbury, Bucks. Marries James L. Haynes-Dixon in London. Visits America for first time.

1950 Revisits India for filming of *The River* by Jean Renoir.

1953 *Kingfishers Catch Fire* is published. Moves to Whiteleaf, Princes Risborough, Bucks.

1955 *An Episode of Sparrows* and *Hans Christian Andersen* (biography) are published.

1956 Moves to Highgate Village, London.

1958 *The Greengage Summer* is published.

1960 Becomes a grandmother.

1961 *China Court* is published.

1962 Moves to Little Douce Grove, Northiam, East Sussex.

1963 *The Battle of the Villa Fiorita* is published.

1964 Revisits India, then returns to England to renovate Hartshorn House, a fifteenth-century dwelling, as new home at Rye, Sussex, after destruction of Little Douce by fire the previous year.

1966 *Two under the Indian Sun,* Godden's first autobiography, written with her sister Jon Godden, is published.

1967 Visits the United States in connection with publication of *The Kitchen Madonna*.

1968 *Gone: A Thread of Stories* is published. Moves to Lamb House, Rye.

1969 Visits the United States in connection with publication of *In This House of Brede*.

1972 *The Diddakoi* is published. Wins England's Whitbread Prize for Children's Literature.

1973 James L. Haynes-Dixon dies.

1975 *Mr. McFadden's Hallowe'en* and *The Peacock Spring* are published.

1977 Godden moves to Scotland to be near her daughters.

1978 *The Rocking Horse Secret* is published.

1979   *A Kindle of Kittens* and *Five for Sorrow; Ten for Joy: A Novel* are published.

1981   *The Dragon of Og* and *The Dark Horse* are published.

1984   *Thursday's Children* is published.

1987   *A Time to Dance, No Time to Weep* is published.

1989   *Fu-Dog* and *A House with Four Rooms* are published.

1990   *Coromandel, Sea Change* is published.

1992   *Listen to the Nightingale* is published.

1993   *Great Grandfather's House* is published.

1994   *Pippa Passes* is published.

Acknowledgments

Thanks to: my field editor, Lois R Kuznets, and my editor at Twayne, Anne Kiefer, for their ongoing support, and to the Twayne staff who helped bring this book to publication; to Dr. Carol Moore, Provost of Mercy College and the Faculty Development Committee, for a grant that gave me some extra time to work on the book; to Marlene Barron and her staff at Manhattan's West Side Montessori School for their exceptional understanding of children (and their parents) and for their generosity; to my mother, Helen, for her loving encouragement and support, without which nothing would have been possible; to my daughter, Sabrina, for being herself.

Chapter One

A Woman for All Seasons

To every thing there is a season, and a time
To every purpose under the heaven . . .

Ecclesiastes 3:1–9

A time to every purpose under the heaven—
But not always . . .

Rumer Godden, *A Time to Dance, No Time to Weep*

Rumer Godden's life reveals itself as a remarkable one through each of her three autobiographies. Each is fascinating in itself, demonstrating the truth of Godden's almost regretful comment in a letter to her sister Jon, quoted in *A Time to Dance, No Time to Weep,* that "No-one could love a house, children or animals more than I do but, . . . it's no use denying it, I am not an ordinary woman." For herself and Jon, the need to create stories was more than the "frustration, a longing to 'express themselves'" other women feel but rather a "constant tug of obligation, as in binding yourself by oath." It is "significant," Godden continues, that "the only women poets down the ages who can be called major were single, or . . . married with one child."[1] In tracing Godden's development as a woman and a writer and profiling the tensions between art and daily routine in her life, each autobiography gives brilliant context to her novels and stories for adults and children.

Godden's three autobiographies are *Two under the Indian Sun* (1966), written with her sister Jon; *A Time to Dance, No Time to Weep* (1987); and *A House with Four Rooms* (1989). *Two under the Indian Sun,* which Godden describes as "not an autobiography as much as an evocation of a time that is gone,"[2] begins when Rumer, aged six, and Jon, seven and a half, leave England, where they have spent a gloomy year in their paternal grandmother's house, and rejoin their parents in India. It concludes six years later as the girls prepare to return to England and school. *A Time to Dance, No Time to Weep* picks up where *Two under the Indian Sun* ends, with the girls' arrival in England to what Godden describes as the end of childhood. The book chronicles the horrors of school life in England, the girls' return to India in their late teens, Godden's training for a career as a dance teacher, her marriage, the birth of her children, her numerous crossings between England and India, and her struggles as a single parent and a writer when abandoned in India by her army officer husband. It concludes with Godden and her children, having lost most of their possessions, heading back to England, where "we could start over again" (243). *A House with Four Rooms* begins as the author and her two children arrive in England in August 1945. It describes Godden's dread of her children's experiencing an alienation similar to that of her own childhood in England, a dread that carries her across the gap of time since her last autobiography. This memoir describes her divorce, remarriage, and family life, her rather glittering literary and social life, and the writing background and context of numerous books. It concludes with her move to Scotland to live near her now grown daughters.

As in her novels, Godden is in her autobiographies extraordinarily sensitive to the perceptions and feelings of children. Describing her autobiographies in *Women's Studies,* Thomas Dukes remarks that so intertwined are the events of Godden's life with her art that the terms "autobiography" and "fiction" are problematic when evaluating her work.[3] Dukes recognizes that Godden's "meta-story" in both novels and autobiographies is one of "female development" and that her comments on "the place of women" make her "autobiographies compelling" (18). Equally compelling, I suggest, is Godden's awareness of the emotional impact on children as they are shunted about to suit their elders' needs or perceptions of what is best for them. This underlying consciousness of the child's often unarticulated responses makes Godden's autobiographies brilliantly colored bildungsromans.

Two under the Indian Sun

Born 10 December 1907 in Sussex, Margaret Rumer Godden was the second of Arthur Leigh Godden and Katherine Norah Hingley's four daughters, who also included Jon, the eldest by sixteen months, and Nancy and Rose, the two younger daughters. Fa, as Godden calls Arthur Godden, worked for a shipping company in India and was responsible for clearing and marking the channels of India's rivers. He preferred managerial posts in small river towns to higher positions in large cities that might have proven more profitable. Following the custom of sending English girls home for education, in 1913 their parents sent Rumer and Jon to live with their five maiden aunts at their paternal grandmother's home at No. 4 Randolph Gardens, Maida Vale, London. There, the girls, despite what Rumer describes as the aunts' goodness, nobility, and dedication, suffered terribly in the formal, solemn, High Anglican religious household where laughter never resounded. They shared the aunts' "straitened circumstances," and although they did not know what that term meant, there seemed to be a "straight hard line drawn each side of their lives, penning them in" (6).

In studying the portraits on her grandmother's wall, Rumer learned about her paternal lineage. Godden was a common Sussex name, derived from the greeting "Good den" that her yeomen ancestors gave one another (French overlords of the time dubbed the Sussex men "Goddens"). But more illustrious than her grandfather's lineage of good yeoman stock was her grandmother's, for it included her great-grandfather Professor Thomas Hewitt Key, who had gone to America as a professor of mathematics, but returned when he learned he'd have to buy slaves if he wished to have servants. Back in England, he became a professor of comparative grammar at London University and one of the founders of University College School.

Another forebear by marriage was Jared Leigh, a painter, one of whose daughters married Rumer Godden's great-great-grandfather, Richard Ironmonger Troward (his portrait as an archer by Benjamin West was displayed in the drawing room of the aunts' house). He was a wealthy patron of the arts and an attorney who prepared on the very mahogany table that stood between the aunts' windows the brief for the prosecution in the trial of Warren Hastings, the English statesman impeached in 1788 and acquitted in 1795 for corruption and cruelty in his administration of India. A portrait by Richard Cosway of Troward's wife holding a baby hung above the fireplace, and the girls were unable to fathom that that baby was the very same grandma they knew, and that she had married Professor Key.

On the maternal side of Rumer's family were the Quaker Hingleys, originally from France. Their mother's grandfather Noah invented a hammer that revolutionized the iron industry. Rumer was named after her maternal grandmother, Harriet Rumer Moore Hingley, whose origins were somewhat mysterious (bringing to mind the young women of mysterious origins that appear often in Godden's books). A reprieve from this ancestral home came to the Godden children after only eighteen months in England, when the threat of zeppelin raids during World War I led to their being recalled to India. As Godden remarks on their feelings aboard the boat carrying them across the ocean, the two girls were really being "recalled" to themselves—the symbolic gesture being when their mother's sister Mary tossed their ugly hats overboard, making the girls feel once again "almost like real children" (14).

Arriving at Narayangunj, where they would spend the next five years, the girls experienced the pleasant shock of seeing their house with its old verandah and of smelling the scents of the garden and bazaar and the jute works across the road. It was a sensory awakening and a sense of coming home to the river country where they belonged. As Godden remarks, "our lives were conditioned by big rivers" (27). Now the girls reveled with their sisters in "avenues of time"; there was no school, and "we were not continually brisked along, as happens to most children of school age" (79). Like Wordsworth's "real children" in "The Prelude," children in India, as Godden and her sister report, are "largely left to grow; principles are gently inculcated, not forced" (11). The children "tried" governesses in "both senses of the word" (68), and their only tutor was their Aunt Mary, who despite her lack of formal education, taught them piano, spelling, grammar, some French, arithmetic, the Bible, and history (*Little Arthur's History of England*). In addition, their mother read them Shakespeare, Shelley, and other writers not traditionally prescribed for children.

Childhood in Narayangunj for Rumer and her sisters was a halcyon time, in which the house's garden reverberated with children's voices and games. Sometimes Jon's scary games, like *Iurchi,* in which the goal was to terrify each other, succeeded so well that neighborhood children would dread visiting the household. At other times, the Godden children left the confines of their garden to wander in the bazaar, meeting with a flood of images that nourished their imaginations—"What would it be like to be a Hindu and go and worship in that temple where the priest was waving a little tray of lights in front of the god doll figures? What would it be like to be that family, father and sons, sitting on a mat spread in front of their hut . . . while the wife and mother stood in the shadows watching? . . . What was it like to be that small boy slipping through the dusk?" (82)

During this time Rumer, while not observing any religion, gained a respect for all religions based on her father's stern statement when she offended a Hindu by repeating the name of his god: "Gods are God . . . When you are in someone else's country you will respect what they respect—and not trespass," Fa admonished her. "Trespass," to "do something hurtful to someone else or something of theirs" (99)—the word haunted Rumer, and so it was with all words. In her article "On Words," Godden muses on her fascination with language, tracing it back through the blood, perhaps to her grammarian grandfather Key, whom she never knew. In the autobiographical *Two under the Indian Sun,* she observes that Hindustani itself was a "vivid language, its words expressive. . . . Unconsciously, we must have thought from English to Hindi, Hindi to English, and, too, were early made aware of the infinite variety of language" (195).

Rumer Godden came from a home in which "all of us wrote; poems and stories poured out of us. . . . Where did this passion come from?" she asks in *Two under the Indian Sun* (195). Exposure to different languages and to a large vocabulary, based on Bible readings and memorizations from *The Book of Common Prayer* with her aunts at Randolph Gardens, and readings aloud from the *Times* and Dickens's *Dombey and Son,* were, she concludes, in part responsible. In addition, Godden remarks, "The poems we learned gave us new words too—we had developed a passion for poetry—as did our Shakespeare readings with Mam and, less approved, the slang we picked up from the young men who came out to the jute works. It went deeper than a surface interest: words could be said to be in our bones— were we not descended from Buttons, our own Professor of Philology— while Fa could make a story out of nothing, or almost nothing" (196). The Godden girls also read through the library in the Narayangunj Club (a social club) or, more accurately, its annex; this is where the women were relegated, but, felicitously, it also housed the books.

In her early teens Rumer had responded to an ad from a publisher (Mr. X) asking for poems. She had borrowed £15 from her mother to pay for their publication. But from early childhood, the Goddens were "true dyed-in-the-wool writers, of the kind who, published or not, would compulsively go on writing" (197). Rumer wrote hymns at age five, and Jon and Rumer each wrote books, Jon illustrating hers. Sometimes the two elder girls wrote together or created extravagant fantasies about the lives of "Big Girls," in which the sisters owned, among other things, "a town and country house, a castle in Scotland, a villa in the South of France, a ranch in Arizona" (201).

Increasingly, the girls also had more solitary writing experiences. "We had think places, private and recognized: Jon's on the roof, Rumer's in what she called the Secret Corner . . . a space under the roof stairs." They soon discovered, however, that "like snails, we could take our think houses with us anywhere," like an invisible tent, and that they "needed to be secret even from one another because we were 'with book' or poem or painting, as if a seed, or perhaps 'grit' is a better simile, had lodged itself in our minds" (203–4).

Both girls constantly created, but Jon was considered the family tal-ent (she was an artist) and the center of parental encouragement. Her father told Jon how and what to draw and gave her extra art classes, disregarding expert advice that she be given no art classes to interfere with her natural talent until she was old enough to go to the Slade Art Institute. As a result of all the extra attention, Rumer conjectures, Jon lost her authenticity as an artist and never achieved her potential. That Rumer was more ignored, her "scribbles" always dismissed as "just Rumer," no one attempting to "blow them up into talent or promise" (209), may have enabled her to grow more as a writer and may be responsible for an underlying sense in her novels that children who are not constantly pushed to perform may be more able to develop resources of their own than those who, like Crystal in Godden's fictional *Thursday's Children,* are too much the focus of vicarious parental pride.

Although, in looking back at her childhood, Rumer Godden recognized the positive aspects of some degree of benign neglect, the preponderance of emotionally or physically abandoned children in her work suggests Godden's ongoing concern with the question of how children manage to develop their own resources in the absence of parental presence. While the Goddens were, as the author remarks in *Two under the Indian Sun,* a "close and doting family," the children experienced many painful separations when they were sent to England, separations that they could not help experiencing as abandonment. Nevertheless, for the mother, the children came first, as attested to by Fa's tall tale of how "one night, as Mam slept on the verandah . . . a man-eating tiger came and seized her, and all Mam said was, 'Eat me quietly and don't wake the children'" (83). Looking back on this tale in *Two under the Indian Sun,* Godden remarks on it as an insight into Fa's loneliness and his distance from his children. Fa was mainly interested in hunting, fishing, and the club. As she recalls, "except for Sunday hide-and-seek he never played with us" (83). Moreover, Fa was insensitive to the hurt he inflicted on Rumer by calling her plain (Jon was the acknowledged beauty); writing about herself in the third person, the author comments, "Rumer and Fa . . . perhaps loved but did not like one another" (196).

In the course of *Two under the Indian Sun,* one sees Godden begin to integrate unhappiness and even evil into her concept of "truthful" writing as she develops resources as an independent thinker and creator. For example, one time, jealous because her sister Nancy's pet rabbit had bunnies and hers had none, she placed two of the young rabbits in her rabbit Connie's hutch, only to see Connie (unbenownst to her, a he-rabbit), devour the animals. "Being stupid and ignorant, it seemed, could do as much harm as being wicked," she writes (135). She exhibits a generalized sense that animals and children are helpless, subject to others' whims.

When Fa shoots his dog Sally, who had broken her leg and so cries through the night, the children tell him, "We'll never trust you again." They sense that Fa killed the dog because he couldn't stand her crying and are struck by adult hypocrisy—that adults tell children not to lie, but lie themselves. This "small death" broke the children's "unquestioning faith in Fa and Ma," Godden observes, and introduced them to the shadowy land between innocence and experience. As a nanny observes to the children, "all of us is Abel . . . and all of us is Cain" (154).

Other shadowings colored the children's consciousness: the omnipresence of death—"we knew without being told, that in India, death was as casual as life" (147)—and a generalized sense of panic at growing up, a feeling that you can't stop "days or rivers," that "willy-nilly, we were growing up even if at times we didn't want to." Everything seemed "broken into" (214), no longer peaceful. When the girls returned from the Hills where they'd vacationed, Narayangunj seemed smaller to them: "'Well, you are older now,' said Mam" (212). Then there appeared Henry, a civilian who had joined the army and lost a leg. His presence as a worker in the jute works and his constant pain repelled them, but Mam refused to allow them to avoid recognizing his anguish. "The world is full of hurt men and women, children dying of hunger . . . it doesn't hurt you to think of it" (215), she admonished her children. The young Rumer's question, "Why should there be a Henry," or "if there has to be, why should he want to come here?" (216) will reverberate in many forms through the author's later works. It appeared in her underlying concern with *darshan,* the Indian word for "looking," for "bearing witness to the world." A character in *An Episode of Sparrows* states that we are each put on earth to bear witness to pain and to try to alleviate it.

At the end of *Two under the Indian Sun,* the sense of broken peace intensifies when Jon and Rumer have a physical fight over Mr. Silcock. The twelve- and thirteen-year-old girls both admire him, but he has eyes only for Jon. As the fight becomes "hurtful, fierce, bitter" (235), moving them further away from childhood, the book concludes, as it began, with the girls on board a ship, five years later, this time England-bound. Their parents are accompanying them to Randolph Gardens to install them in school, as was the custom among English colonial families.

A Time to Dance, No Time to Weep

Here *A Time to Dance, No Time to Weep* begins, as the children, filled with dread at the prospect of returning to a gloomy England, watch their luggage being unloaded on the quay at Plymouth. After placing the girls in boarding school, Fa departs for India and Mam remains in England. With its strict nuns, discipline (the "spirit must be broken"), sparse food, and lack of warmth, St. Monica's was a hellhole for the children, accustomed as they were to life under the Indian sun. This was the first time they had the sense "a father and mother could be against their children"; how could they say, "you will get used to it, then you will like it"? (23) When the children refused to write home because the nuns read their mail, their mother became alarmed; and when a friend visited and saw their poor health and misery, they were fetched home.

Although the nuns had allowed no secret space for writing or keeping notes, the misery of that time is recorded in Godden's short story "The Little Fishes" in the collection *Gone* and in her novel *Black Narcissus. A Time to Dance, No Time to Weep* is rich in sources for Godden's later work. The children attended five schools in the next two years, living with Mam in Eastbourne, in a succession of "shoddy houses" to which they were ashamed to invite school friends. Eastbourne, to Rumer, represented the "epitome of mediocrity," everything "middle, middle, middle," inflaming a longing for London (26). To counteract the frustrations of their isolated life, Mam took the children on a trip to the battlefields of France. The ostensible reason for the trip was to make the children think of those who nobly gave their lives for others and thereby render them less selfish. Another reason, however, may have been Mam's maternal sense that the children needed the excitement of a trip. The trip to Chateau Thierry, a town on the Marne, during which Mam became ill and the girls had to fend for themselves, became the basis of *The Greengage Summer.* On this trip, the children were befriended by a man who turned out be a French Canadian spy and by a family whose members were really unmarried thieves with a hired or borrowed "daughter." This experience of meeting people who were not what they seemed further changed the two elder girls, introducing both to complex questions of good, evil, love, and forgiveness and Rumer to the unwilling recognition that Jon was growing more mature and apart from her.

Rumer's role as a writer became clearer to her at Moira House, the school at which she encountered Mona Swann, an English teacher with high standards who recognized how true talent must be nurtured. Exercises in writing summaries, literary and linguistic comparisons, and a specialized reading program honed Godden's skills and provided a complement to an already developed sense that "truthful writing" consists of that in which "credibility was not distorted or manipulated, even in fantasies" (48). At Moira House, Rumer felt transported from

Eastbourne into a world as a writer, a world in which she felt "chosen." This feeling that is expressed in terms of dance in her books on ballet in which the children admitted to Queen's Chase Academy experience a sense of nobility that transcends social class.

Following graduation from Moira House at seventeen, Godden had her first experience of "love"—with a woman a year younger than she. Shelagh was "tall, cool, almost laconic" (49). As the author comments, in the 1920s same-sex love was not widely recognized, and their relationship continued undisturbed until Godden's decision to join her mother and Jon to return to India. Entering the Calcutta social season, Godden became engaged to and then disengaged from her father's coworker Ian, who, she remarks in *A Time to Dance, No Time to Weep,* compared poorly with her ideal of Mr. Darcy in *Pride and Prejudice* (56).

The following years saw Godden using a small legacy left by her godfather to train herself to become a teacher of dance despite a childhood leg injury. Godden's interest in teaching focused on children: "I only wanted to give ordinary, everyday children a chance to dance for the joy of it, and did not aspire to teach anyone over the age of ten or eleven. . . . I have seen shy children transformed by dancing, inhibited children released and, incidentally, faults of posture, legs and feet helped and cured, but I knew, if I were to teach at all, it must be honest—what could be called 'truthful dancing'" (74).

During the crowded social season, Rumer Godden met Laurence Sinclair Foster, whom she describes as a "cheerful Philistine," a brilliant athlete with no interest in culture. Rumer became pregnant, and her entire being reacted against abortion. Responding to her father's "Olympian ways," as a young girl, Rumer had prayed, "Please God, let me grow up good enough to be like the Virgin Mary and have a baby without being married" (56). Nonetheless, in 1934 Godden married Foster; from the outset she felt the marriage was a pretense, although she enjoyed its social aspects. Rumer Godden's first novel, *Chinese Puzzle,* inspired by her lifelong love of Pekingese dogs, describes an ancient Chinese man's reincarnation as a dog in contemporary England. It was accepted in 1935 by the publisher Curtis Brown on the same day Godden's daughter Jane was born at her paternal grandfather's house in a London suburb, while Laurence was on leave. Shortly thereafter, Laurence returned to Calcutta, leaving his new daughter behind and his wife to cope as well as she could as a single parent. Although *Chinese Puzzle* was well-reviewed, it did not do well in sales. Nor did her second book, *The Lady and the Unicorn,* a story in which the daughters of a

Eurasian family living in Calcutta are obsessed by their house's suppos-
edly ghostly inhabitants and misled by their upper-class English
boyfriends. The themes of these relatively unsuccessful early works—the
hidden links between the generations—will reappear more successfully
in later works, such as *A Fugue in Time* and *China Court,* justifying Curtis
Brown's farsighted advice to Godden to ignore criticism and follow her
"natural inclination . . . just write whatever the spirit moves you to
write" (117).

Believing she should be with her husband, Godden left England with
Jane, but felt a misfit in Laurence's Calcutta. She returned to England in
time for her second daughter, Paula Janaki, to be born in 1938, com-
pleting her third book, *Black Narcissus,* on the ocean voyage from India.
A period of deep depression and suicidal thoughts followed, triggered by
her baby's frailty and thoughts of her beloved doctor's suicide in
Calcutta, "of what was happening to Jews like him as the evil of
Nazidom spread over the world, and it seemed it was not one to bring
children into." Recalling her thoughts of "hiring a caravan to take Jane,
Paula and myself up to some remote place on the moor and ending
everything by setting fire to it," Godden comments that although she is
ashamed of these feelings, she knows that her experience with "that
abyss" has "helped me to understand other people's hopelessness" (130).

Black Narcissus, which helped rescue Godden from her depression, was
published in 1939 to some success. It is the story of a group of Anglican
nuns who fail in their attempt to establish a school and hospital at a
general's palace at Mopu.

Gypsy, Gypsy, Godden's next novel, published in 1940, is another tale
of the struggle between innocence and experience. Here the evil
Madame Barbe de Longuemarie envies her young niece and, through a
convoluted series of maneuvers, takes pleasure in depriving a spirited
Gypsy of his freedom. *Gypsy, Gypsy*'s moderate success increased
Godden's reputation in the literary world, confirming for her "the belief
I had cherished so long in secret, that I was born to be a writer" (136).
The proceeds of publication went in part to support Laurence, who, back
in India, failed to pay bills.

Crossing the sea again, Godden and her daughters returned to
Calcutta, this time with a Swiss-Italian nanny, Giovanna. Little is said of
Laurence in *A Time to Dance, No Time to Weep;* Rumer Godden was
focused on writing book number five, *Breakfast with the Nikolides,* to be
published in 1942. This book, set in India, describes a young girl, her
sister, and her mother who join the father in India. *Breakfast with the*

Nikolides, Godden observes, is "nearest to our 'truthful writing'" (161). This book in which a woman becomes increasingly estranged from her husband may reflect Godden's own increasing frustrations at Laurence's erratic behavior. Laurence, she discovered, after impulsively joining the army, had gambled and lost everything, selling the house, car, and children's educational policies. In 1942, Godden was left on her own to pay off his debts.

Godden took the children to Kashmir, where, as an "abandoned family," she received a small stipend and suffered extreme hardship as a single parent. In Kashmir she taught dancing, wrote, mothered her often seriously ill children, suffered a miscarriage, and lived on a houseboat—all against the backdrop of the war in Europe. Hospitalized with influenza and jaundice, Godden saw that she had been like a bird trapped in a net, struggling to escape. In a revelation reminiscent of Wordsworth's in his sonnet "Composed on Westminster Bridge," Godden began to see a "hole of escape" in stillness. Like a character in her novel *Kingfishers Catch Fire,* she determined, "instead of living to get money to spend," to live by "not spending" (184).

In January 1943, she rented Dove House, in a remote part of Kashmir, and lived there under spare (but not "straitened") circumstances. There Godden had a beautiful papier-mâché lamp "painted with Kingfishers in deep rich colours" (190); it was around this image that she developed *Kingfishers Catch Fire.* As the world outside crumbled with family misfortunes and the war, Dove House remained a sanctuary.

At Dove House, which had a sense of timelessness, Godden studied and was fascinated by "Dunne's Theory of Time in which time is all one, not divided into past, present and future" (194). She wrote to Jon, asking her to send copies of Wordsworth's poems and of Virginia Woolf's *Orlando,* works concerned with the transcendence of time. During this period at Dove House she wrote *A Fugue in Time,* published in America as *Take Three Tenses. A Fugue in Time* is a book in which voices from three time periods speak. To make this choreography work, she rewrote the manuscript eight times, until she found the key. As she remarks in *A Time to Dance, No Time to Weep,* "by putting the past into the present, the present into the past, it worked, and more remarkably, no-one, not even the critics noticed the shifts; the whole had miraculously blended" (216).

Godden's wish that the components of her life would also miraculously blend was not to be fulfilled for long. For a short while at Dove House, Godden felt that the war had set out to teach her "to become an ordinary woman" and to overcome what one critic referred to as her "horror of the commonplace" (217). This "horror," Godden admits, developed in part through her Raj (upper-class) upbringing in India, where even the poorest British had servants, and in her reaction to middle-class Randolph Gardens and Eastbourne. At Dove House, she necessarily engaged in the homely tasks of sewing, cooking, and dealing with servants and children under primitive conditions, exercises that would, she hoped, improve her skills in conducting ordinary life.

Home life was disrupted when Godden agreed to share Dove House with a neighboring female painter, Olwen. In so doing, she felt she had sacrificed "the whole concept and truth of Dove House." Now Olwen redid the house, ordered the servants about, and insisted that the children dine separately, saying, "You see . . . it only needed a firm hand. Now I can paint in peace and you can write" (225). Godden's daughter Jane became the model for Teresa, who, when peace begins to dissolve in *Kingfishers Catch Fire,* refers to one room in the house as the "Quarrelling Room." Now Godden's den became the "Quarrelling Room." When asked to write a poem, ten-year-old Jane wrote, "Two little bulbuls were sitting on a wall / Quarrelling and pecking, quarrelling and pecking . . . / This is more than flesh and blood can stand" (225). Other incidents at Dove House parallel to those in *Kingfishers Catch Fire,* such as Godden's estrangement from the villagers and the poisoning of the household's food by a servant (in real life, Rumer's housemate, Olwen, nearly died).

Godden's novels typically offer possibilities of redoings and redemption much harder to come by in first-and-only-time-around-life. In real life, the servant was a homicidal maniac preying on vulnerable women; in *Kingfishers Catch Fire,* he is portrayed as a far more complex and sympathetic figure who believes he is giving the character a "potion" to cause her to fall in love with him. In *Kingfishers Catch Fire,* the servant is forgiven. Godden's attitude toward Olwen's near-killer was much less generous, and she never saw Olwen again.

A Time to Dance, No Time to Weep ends as it began, with Godden and her children arriving in 1944 on the quay in England, this time at Liverpool. Godden carries two important possessions: a valuable Agra rug she bought from "Profit David," a cunning but kind rug merchant; and the completed manuscript of *The River.*

A House with Four Rooms

A House with Four Rooms begins as Godden and her young family are about to start a new life. Godden, now thirty-eight, Jane (nine), and

Paula (six) arrive at Liverpool and the author ruminates that "every book I write, a novel, a memoir, that is even remotely connected with our family begins the same way," with the family "alighting in a stranger place to start a new life, probably in a new way" (17). Laurence has not been seen in two years, Godden's possessions (save the rug and manuscript) are in a Bombay warehouse, and Godden and Paula have been deathly ill on the trip over.

As Godden comments throughout her work, neither time nor the river stands still and movement seems endemic to her life. As the epigraph to the book suggests, the name of her third memoir derives from an "Indian proverb or axiom that says that everyone is a house with four rooms, a physical, a mental, an emotional and a spiritual. Most of us tend to live in one room most of the time, but unless we go into every room every day, even if only to keep it aired, we are not a complete person." *A House with Four Rooms* details the ways in which the author continues to visit each of these rooms.

Arriving at Darrynane near Bodmin, where her parents now lived, Godden was shocked by their aged appearance but reassured to find furniture and treasures remembered from her own childhood. Past and present flowed together in her life as they do in her fiction. The structure of *A House with Four Rooms* is itself more complex than the earlier memoirs, as past, present, and future strands interweave with Godden reviewing earlier days, looking ahead to the births of her grandchildren and filling in the events of her new life in London. This new life will focus on her raising her children, her divorce and remarriage, and the literary and social events revolving around the publication of her books.

Moving to London with the children, Godden, after some agonizing, sent Jane and Paula to boarding school and was therefore free to devote herself to her writing. As she remarks, "though indeed I would miss Jane and Paula acutely and perhaps loved them more than ever, it was a strange mingling of triumph and achievement; the schools could give them what I could not and now, at last, I could, I thought, come into the literary world where I belonged, and, too, find London" (48).

In Godden's use of the word "perhaps" in the above quotation, her decision to put her own writing first because she was pregnant "with book" (54), and her failure to look closely into the conditions of her children's scarcely described schooling (curious, given her own miserable school experiences), one may detect a struggle underlying many of the author's novels. Mothers in *The Battle of the Villa Fiorita* and in *Kingfishers Catch Fire,* feeling overwhelmed by motherhood, make choices that in effect lead them to abandon their children in order to develop their own resources "willy-nilly," for better or worse. As will be seen, Godden's fictional children almost always draw on and develop unexpected and remarkable strengths in all four rooms of the self. Harder to determine is what the unaccounted "rent" paid by them for living in those rooms at such an early age may be.

When Godden's children came home for the holidays, Godden engaged the unpleasant Mrs. Errington, a nanny from "Proxy Parents." When eleven-year-old Jane claimed, "I can look after Paula and Simon [Godden's nephew] better than that" (55), Godden felt she was right, but "eleven years old was not quite old enough to brave a totally unknown London and I had to harden my heart, trying not to see those two pairs of eyes, aquamarine and blue, demanding, 'How can you do this to us?' Jane's worry frown had come back. 'Suppose Paula runs away?'" "She's got plenty of sense," Godden replied. "She would probably get in a taxi and come home" (56). In critical, self-sufficient, stalwart and sensible Paula and Jane, we see models of Godden's fictional children, who brave the byways of Kashmir, Italy, and London on their own to achieve their self-defined goals.

Before long, however, Godden came to "feel cruel about leaving the children in unsatisfactory schools," and both children were finally placed in Moira House, where Godden took up study again with Mona Swann. Moira House was also a boarding school, and Godden's intensifying pain over sacrificing the children on behalf of her work, even to a superior boarding school, became clear when she spoke to Swann about her conflict between her need to write and the children's wish to go to a day school. Swann replied, "If you give in, would either job be done properly?" Though Godden concurred that "they would not," she wondered, "was it all a mistake?" and then recalled "the night before the children went, I heard them talking in bed. 'I do wish,' said Paula, 'that man's wife had never picked that apple.' 'Why?' asked Jane. 'Without it,' said Paula, 'there wouldn't have been any schools'" (81).

Much of this third memoir is focused on Godden's marriage in 1949 to the emotionally supportive (but later emotionally vulnerable) James Haynes-Dixon and their lives in various homes; and on her relations with her publishers, especially Curtis Brown and Harold Macmillan, and with directors of various films of her books, particularly with Jean Renoir, who filmed *The River.* Also remembered is her encounter with Christianity in her later years, when she found, in the nuns at Stanbrook Abbey, a silence and concentration that filled a deep need. While she could not take communion because of her divorce, she felt spiritually at home at last, and then wrote *In This House of Brede*, a novel that presents a positive portrait of a group of nuns' spiritual growth within their convent.

But perhaps the most fascinating aspect of *A House with Four Rooms* is the insight it offers into Godden's writing process. *The River* and *The Mousewife* were "vouchsafed," the latter written in fifty-five minutes with no words changed. In contrast, *Kingfishers Catch Fire* and *An Episode of Sparrows* were written at Pollard House, where Godden lived so happily with James in the 1950s that she felt she was not "in" the books or "they in me" (161).

The complicated *China Court* was written in Old Hall, London (where Godden had relocated in the late 1950s to remove Jane from the fast-paced social life of the nursing school she was attending near Pollards House). Now that Godden had perfected her technique of mixing tenses, *China Court,* modeled in part on Darrynane, took only eighteen months to write. *The Battle of the Villa Fiorita* was written "because I had grown tired of the innumerable novels . . . about child victims of divorce" (216). In that book the children fight back, going to fetch their mother home from Italy where she's fled with her lover. It is interesting to conjecture how the glittering social life attendant on her London publishing success and the translation of her books into films may have symbolized to Godden temptation and the potentially negative side of art that conflicts with family life.

In 1972, Godden won the Whitbread Prize for children's literature for *The Diddakoi,* a book about a Gypsy child in an English village. Looking back on her work, Godden remarks in *The House with Four Rooms* that "there are two things in my long working life that have perhaps been of use and have also given me pure pleasure" (298).

On her first "pure pleasure," her work in children's literature, Godden writes, "I have always been fascinated by the miniature." It is a fascination that once led her to sell her only warm coat to buy a dolls' house. "My books for children," she comments, "are about small things, dolls' house size dolls, pocket dolls, mice" (161). *The Dolls' House,* a success when it appeared in 1947, was picked up for a television series in the 1980s. The production made "television history" because, as Godden explains in *A House with Four Rooms,* "it was not acted by cartoons or puppets but by dolls who moved by electronic controls" (162). As Godden recalls, when parents complained that children were deeply upset by the demise of a character, the producer commented, "Children often have to learn about death and if you had told your little daughter to stop sobbing and listen to what Tottie said afterwards, she would have gone to bed comforted and wiser." John Betjeman called *The Dolls' House* "a little masterpiece," and Godden concurs, feeling that like *The Mousewife* and *The River*, it was "vouchsafed" (162). She has, Godden tells us, since tried to write a children's book between each two novels or biographies.

The second "pure pleasure" derives from the poetry recitals Godden initiated in the late 1970s, leading to her becoming known to children as "the poetry lady" (298). Godden's readings for the BBC, at libraries (she was especially pleased when a library in Winona, Wisconsin, was named in her honor) and in schools were intended to "show children that poetry is meant for pleasure, exploration, entertainment, as well as learning" (299). Children were transported by the writings of Shakespeare, Milton, Chaucer, Wordsworth, Gerard Manley Hopkins, and Dylan Thomas, and Godden was not surprised.[4] "Children are naturals for poetry" because "they and poets are akin," Godden says, quoting the words of Professor Dover Wilson in *The Shakespearean Scholar*:

> Upon this planet there dwell two strange races of people. The first is a tribe small of stature and delicate of limb . . . our eyes are lamps in which the oil of reason burns, their eyes are charmed casements through which the moon of imagination pours—until we teach them to forget. . . . Yet there are a few, a very few, who do not forget . . . they are the true creators . . . they bring cosmos or beauty into a world which is without form and void. And so they have the name "Makers or Poets." (*Four Rooms*, 301)

In 1973, James died, leaving Godden in a depression that lasted till 1977. Comforted by her omnipresent Pekingese and by "small things," Godden continued to write, even at seventy wandering shady Parisian quarters from midnight until 3 A.M. (followed by a friend in a taxi) to research *Five for Sorrow; Ten for Joy*, a novel about a brothel and nuns. Soon after, Godden moved to Scotland to be near her married daughters, while "still not too old to adjust" (312). In Scotland, she has continued to write, as she promised, alternating books for adults and books for children. Readers may yet anticipate a fourth autobiography, detailing the life she has lived while writing her more recent novels.

If Godden's memoirs describe a peripatetic life in which she has rarely lived in one house for very long, it is a life in which she has spent a great deal of time in each room of the house fundamental to the Indian proverb, rooms into which she has graciously invited her many devoted readers to wander and thereby refurbish their own.

In her epilogue to *A House with Four Rooms,* Godden concludes by referring to the physical, mental, emotional, and spiritual rooms of the self: "All of us tend to inhabit one room more than another but I have tried to go most days into them all—each has its riches. My house is, of course, slightly worn now but I still hope to go on living quietly in all of it, finding treasures, old and new until the time comes when I shall have, finally, to shut its door" (314).

Chapter Two

Excursions in Time, Space, and Spirit, 1942–1948

Godden's image of the self as a "house with four rooms" is an apt one for her work as well as her life, for her novels take readers on excursions through internal and external time and space as well as into realms of the spirit.

By the time Godden's first novel with a child protagonist, *Breakfast with the Nikolides,* appeared in 1942, Godden had already published *Chinese Puzzle* (1936), *The Lady and the Unicorn* (1938), *Black Narcissus* (1939), and *Gypsy, Gypsy* (1940), each of these exploring the house of the self from a different perspective. *Chinese Puzzle,* with its canine, formerly human protagonist, examines the consequences of action and inaction on the human being's physical and spiritual shape and on the creation of a writer; *The Lady and the Unicorn* explores the continuity or lack of it between past and present; *Gypsy, Gypsy* probes the nature of physical, mental, emotional, and spiritual cruelty; and *Black Narcissus* presents a picture of failed spirituality. While all of these early themes run through Godden's later work, the first three figure most strongly in Godden's novels of the 1940s, in which childhood holds center stage.

In *Breakfast with the Nikolides, Take Three Tenses* (originally *A Fugue in Time,* 1945), *The River* (1946), and *The Dolls' House* (1947), children (and dolls) experience difficulty in moving between the rooms of the self. The tension expressed in the emotional and physical cruelty between a mother and daughter, a tension that intensifies when the mother destroys her daughter's dog, is the compelling force in *Breakfast with the Nikolides,* as is the fierce sense of how this tension can serve as a catalyst in the making of a writer. In *Take Three Tenses,* the childhood house to which an old man returns represents his hope for continuity and for the salving of unresolved childhood and adolescent pain. In *The River,* a young girl is challenged to accept change and to integrate the pain that comes with growth into her vision of herself as a female and a writer. In *The Dolls' House,* the house becomes a framework that permits not only the dolls but their human mistresses to wish for and to some degree to achieve integration of the self. Finally, in *A Candle for St. Jude,* Godden's first book with a balletic theme, ballet, like writing, becomes a means by which the self finds its spiritual as well as its physical home.

Breakfast with the Nikolides

Fleeing World War II, Rumer Godden had brought her two daughters to India in 1939. Louise Pool, in *Breakfast with the Nikolides,* also escapes the European war, bringing her children—Emily, age eleven; and Binnie, eight—to India. She has been separated from her husband, Charles, for eight years, and their reunion is marked by a tension that will overflow into Louise's relationship with her elder daughter. The ways in which mother and daughter suffer at one another's hands are so intensely described from both perspectives, and the redeeming role of art is so persuasively presented, that the reader may wonder if Godden's personal experience encompassed both child and adult points of view. Whatever the sources of the book, however, it ranks among the most emotionally powerful and best crafted of Godden's early works.

As the ship nears Amorra in East Bengal, Louise Pool looks down at the water and sees a ghost of herself. Overtaken by memories and nightmares of her last visit to India, she feels her identity washing away in the river, her hat ribbons resolving into "the two long ribbons of steamer wash," the wake of the boat.[1] In the course of the novel, it will emerge that Louise had fled India when her husband took her sexually against her will, leaving her pregnant with their second child.

As the river soothes and calms Emily's mind and she feels herself opening up to a new life, the girl sees her mother's face and wonders what is causing her strange expression. When they meet Charles, he seems awkwardly nervous, but Emily recognizes herself in his rude speech patterns and pities him. She also absorbs her mother's discomfort upon reentering Charles's house; she clutches Emily's shoulder so hard it hurts. When Charles tells Louise she's "made [her] bed and can lie in it," Emily—unlike Binnie, who naively asks, "You needn't ever make your beds in India, need you?" (30)—catches the undertones of sarcasm.

Emily feels overwhelmed by Louise, who claims to know her better than she knows herself and who sees Emily as "hard . . . completely oblivious of everyone but herself . . . she is almost unnatural" (85). Later, thinking of Louise, Emily will recognize how she takes over everything in her mind and paralyzes her with her perceptions, and she makes a determined effort to block her out: "Whenever I start to think . . . I come back to Louise. Now—I shall teach myself to stop thinking of you . . . soon, soon I shall think of myself and not of you, and I shall be free" (94).

A bond develops between Emily and Charles, who senses Emily's need for love and gives her a dog, Don, whose very name suggests "gift." That for Emily Don represents the world is suggested by the Joycean label she affixes to his collar:

DON
POOL
Government Farm
Amorra
Bengal
India
Asia
The World
The Universe (59)

Emily's fierce love for Don is betrayed when Louise, frightened that Don's sudden frenzied behavior might signal rabies, has him destroyed when she sends Emily and Binnie to breakfast at the neighboring home of the Nikolides. Emily senses something is wrong as she gets on the boat that will take her down the river to the Nikolides, and wonders, "What is it? . . . What has mother done?" (104). Indeed, the journey on the river is to be a transition between innocence and experience, for Emily will return a different girl, every vestige of innocence gone.

Louise feels equally frightened by Emily: "I see you too . . . you always do all you possibly can to upset me." Yet Louise confirms Emily's perception of her power over her daughter: "I can turn your thoughts like the wind on a paper streamer" (106), she thinks, referring to the fact that sending Emily off to the much awaited breakfast has had the effect of diverting her mind from Don, whom Emily has not seen that morning.

When Emily returns and misses Don, Louise tells her he has died after becoming rabid in a dogfight. Emily, shocked, refuses to believe that Louise is telling the truth about the way he died or even that he is dead. She torments Louise by insisting Don is alive. She continues to call out to walk and feed the phantom dog, driving Louise further into a hysteria that has progressively deepened with her stay in India. Reliving the rage and boredom that drove her to leave Charles eight years ago, Louise feels she is "being killed by them all, by Charles, and Emily and the remembrance of Don, by the silence and noise of the place, by the heaviness of the sky." No one "could exist here and remain herself," she thinks in despair. "'I am dying, dying, dying,' cried Louise, 'and I do not want to die'" (180).

Emily embarks on a crusade to discover the truth and learns that her mother's hysterical fear of illness has caused her to have Don put down despite the protests of the Indian vet; Louise forbids him to examine the dog before injecting the lethal dose. As Emily's vendetta against Louise continues, Emily is conscious of being changed: "I am not like a child now . . . I am grown up." The trauma of Don's death has, she feels, turned her "old" overnight, and she has difficulty connecting with the carefree girl who dressed up to have breakfast with the Nikolides; indeed, "Breakfast with the Nikolides was always to be the last hour of her childhood" (158).

Emily feels a despair equal to or surpassing her mother's. Holding an empty leash that for her signals a newly emptied universe, "in a rush of despair she thought, 'This is what it feels like to be dead'" (240). Emily maintains an inner monologue as she struggles to absorb Don's death, a reality Charles knows she could have dealt with if told beforehand that Don was truly sick: "He did not die in this untruthful way," Emily thinks to herself. "Somebody had a hand in it, and I think it was you, Louise. You had no right to do it! You cannot take him from me like this. You do it because you think I am a child. I shall keep him alive until I choose to agree he is dead" (159). Now Emily determines to be on guard constantly, to "pay attention." This requires a persistent search for the truth, an undertaking that is central to the role of the artist. Refusing to "blink painful facts," as a young character tries to do in the later novel *The Battle of the Villa Fiorita*, Emily develops a writer's consciousness and voice: "I shall say to myself in the day and in the night, 'pay attention, Emily,' and I have taken a book to my private place in the tomato bed where I shall write everything down in truthful writing" (159–60).

Earlier, because of the tug-of-war between their wills, Emily had teased Louise that she would name her own children "Willy and Nilly." Now, she is pure will. "'Mark you, Louise,' wrote Emily and liked it, 'mark you, I shall get what I want in the end,' that is, the truth" (171). As she sharpens her desire for truth, she is helped by Blake's poetry, which Charles often recites:

Bring me my bow of burning gold,
Bring me my arrows of desire,
Bring me my spear, O clouds unfold,
Bring me my chariot of fire. (90)

While Emily notes, "I have no bows and arrows" or "sword or spear," she promises not to "cease from mental fight till I have found out everything, Louise" (172).

Poetry also helps Emily in the form of Anil, a young Indian student poet who befriends her as she sits alone on a hillside at night, trying to commune with Don's ghost. Anil's sensitivity moves him to comfort the girl by telling her about the Hindu custom of *puja,* whereby prayers and gifts are offered to the dead to lay the soul to rest. He suggests she ask the vet the answers to her questions about what diseases kill dogs and then perform a *puja* for Don. Anil takes Emily home, but Louise, in a peak of hysteria, accuses him of molesting the girl. This triggers a riot among the students, who mistakenly believe Anil has been imprisoned. Anil suddenly dies as a result of an earlier infection, his death intersecting with Don's and confirming Emily's belief that poets die young. Emily, meanwhile, has pursued Anil's suggestion of questioning the vet. In so doing, she has learned the truth of what Louise has done and has formed a new image of a good mother in the vet's wife, Shila. Shila is pregnant and seems kind and accepting, although the reader, not Emily, also sees Shila as ignored and otherwise psychologically abused by her husband.

Now Emily confronts Louise, who has been wishing to find a way to tell Emily the truth but dreads her growing up and out of her control. Armed with the truth, Emily sees Louise as "suddenly quite small" (279). Despite her wish to keep Emily a child, Louise shares her daughter's sense of her own diminution and comments, "Emily, how tall you are!" When Emily tells her she knows the truth, Louise says, "He is dead. . . . It's no good wishing." Emily agrees and even kisses Louise at Louise's request, now "conscious of a new feeling—like stretching, as if she had the power to stretch herself out and touch . . . a new world . . . headlong in its possibilities of loneliness, there was strength and satisfaction in it. . . . 'I am free,'" she thinks (280). This sense of newly acquired self enables her to lay Don to rest with the concluding *puja* she performs for him. The candle, burning steadily as it floats down the river, burns for Don, Anil, Emily, and perhaps even Louise, all at once, for as Anil had said, "if you offer for one you offer for all" (292). Louise herself has reached a rapprochement with Charles, who is a loving father and claims to have lost his temper with his wife only once.

Questions remain at the end of the book. Though Charles is a loving father, today's reader is apt to have difficulty accepting his rationale for losing his temper and raping Louise eight years ago: he did it for a good reason—Louise was trying to make him jealous—and the rape had a good result—the conception of their younger daughter, Binnie. Narayan, the vet, also mistreats his wife by turning a blind eye to her needs and wishes; yet at the end of the book he defines religion as "nonviolence—to be completely without violence to any" (290). The question of Rumer Godden's attitude toward male indifference or occasional violence in marriage is one that will arise from time to time in her work—in *China Court* and in *Listen to the Nightingale,* for example. But if the question of how adults resolve their differences remains, *Breakfast with the Nikolides* closes with the certainty that Emily Pool has looked deeply into the reflecting pool of her own consciousness and will be prepared to face whatever later truths she must with courage, perhaps integrating the imperfect insights of others with a higher level of understanding in her own adult life.

Take Three Tenses

Take Three Tenses continues to explore the truth Emily Pool learns: that all things are interrelated. There is even a line in *Take Three Tenses* quoted from Gertrude Stein that seems to evoke the previous book and serve as a transition between the two: "I am I because my little dog knows me."[2] This phrase exists in the mind of the American-born army officer Grizel Dane. Grizel, the grandniece of Rolls Dane, the elderly occupant of 99 Willoughby Street in London, seeks temporary lodging in her ancestral home. In the course of the book, Grizel will learn that her identity goes far beyond the limits of the self and is enmeshed with the home she has never seen before and that, in a sense, she is known by all the animals and people who have inhabited the Dane house over the past one hundred years.

I am the house dog
I am the house cat
Chick, chick, chick . . .
Take Three Tenses. (165)

Voices from the past, present, and future—the three tenses—speak out of the rafters of the old house in which all time is eternal. First published as *A Fugue in Time, Take Three Tenses* is prefaced by a sentence written by Lawrence Abbott that describes Bach's fugues but also suggests the underlying structure of the novel: "Two, three or four simultaneous melodies which are constantly on the move, each going its own indepen-

dent way. For this reason the underlying harmony is often hard to deci-
pher, being veiled by a maze of passing notes and suspensions. . . . Often
chords are incomplete; only two tones are sounded so that one's imagination has to fill in the missing third tone."

Also prefacing the book are lines from T. S. Eliot's "East Coker,"
which Rolls recites at crucial moments:

Home is where one starts out from. As we grow older
The world becomes stranger, the pattern more complicated
Of dead and living. Not the intense moment
Isolated, with no before and after,
But a lifetime burning in every moment
And not the lifetime of one man only . . .

Two additional epigraphs from *The Book of Common Prayer* refer to the
brevity of life and the importance of children, who are a "heritage and gift
like the arrows in the hand of the giant: even so are the young children."

Rolls Dane is the sole surviving member of his generation of Danes,
living in the house that has been leased to his family for ninety-nine
years. The lease is about to expire without renewal by the owner, and
Rolls, who has spent most of his life elsewhere, now feels deep attach-
ment to his ancestral home, and unwillingness to leave it: "I don't want
the family to go out of the house" (5). Indeed, the identity of the family
is tied to 99 Wiltshire Place. "'In me you exist' says the house" (3). The
original Dane was John Ironmonger, who brought his young bride,
Griselda, to the house in 1841. Together they produced numerous children, including Pelham, Selina, the twins Elizabeth and Frederick (who
die young), and Roly (Rolls's boyhood name).

Dane's mother, Griselda, a woman of independent mind, is unhappy.
As her name suggests, she is patient, not hysterical, and she is outspoken
to her husband. She tells him that he reminds her a little of her father,
whom she never liked, and that she fantasizes running away. John tells
his wife he knows her better than she knows herself. He ignores her
admission that she longs to leave home for adventure and that she fears
punishment for not caring about the children John has imposed on her.
"Nine is my lucky number" (113), John asserts as the number of Danes
increases over twenty-two years, ending only in Griselda's escape
through death at Roly's birth in 1863.

For Griselda, marriage and motherhood have been a death sentence.
"You have never known me," Griselda tells her husband. "All you want

and are determined to have is—an angel in the house" (115). Referring to John as the "Eye" because of his all-knowing stance, Griselda accuses him of treating her like a doll or a child: "I believe you give more respect, John, to the few words a man in the street might say to you, than you do to me when I speak to you with my whole heart. But dolls don't have hearts do they? . . . Nor children? At least not hearts that are big enough to care" (116). Griselda's frustrations as a woman are shared by her daughter Selina, who grows up feeling unloved. Deprived of an education comparable to her brothers' (despite Griselda's intercession) and not permitted to have her own pet, "Lena" grows up embittered and set in her ways. She will be unkind to Lark, the mysterious seven-year-old girl John Dane brings home nine years after his wife's death, claiming she has been orphaned by a train crash. All that is known about Lark's parents is that they were in the theater, the seductive world of the arts. The children in the family are admonished to treat Lark like a sister, and, indeed, the reader may suspect that she is Dane's natural daughter.

Lark is a lonely, unkempt, but vibrant girl who receives little attention from anyone and contempt from Selina. Her wish to have music lessons as she did with her parents is denied, and Selina tells her she is a penniless orphan who ought to be grateful for whatever she receives. When Selina assigns Lark an essay on Africa as punishment for her boldness, Lark asks to write one on Italy instead, quoting sensuous lines from a book on Italian landscape and asserting she'll live there when grown up, despite Selina's crushing remarks. Lark's determination will pay off, for she will marry a marchese and live in Italy. In *Take Three Tenses,* as in *China Court,* only an outsider can retain sufficient detachment and sense of self to escape some of the drearier lessons of the family home.

Rolls, enamored as he now is of the house, has done his best to separate himself from it for much of his life. His life unfolds in three stages: as a child and as a young and then an old man. As a child, he is known as Roly and delights in learning the "difficult" names of flowers, even wishing he were a girl to avoid becoming a soldier. Like Lark, though, he is tormented by the negative surrogate mother image of Selina, who exerts on them the control she lacks over her own future. She insists that he will indeed become a soldier and urges him on in his lessons: "Take three tenses . . . past, present and future." When Roly resists the grammatical review, Selina parses for him: "Even a little boy like you has a past, a present and a future. You were a baby, you are a boy, you will be a man." Roly sees further than that as a child—"But I am always here,

Lena. Like they say at school, 'Present.' I am always present so why not only one?" (42)

Now an old man, Rolls no longer remembers the difficult Latin names of flowers. Facts have become too harsh for him to absorb (the fact of losing the house, for example). In his mind he has again become the soldier Selina decreed he would, who yielded to Selina's insidious if prudent advice that he postpone marrying Lark till his salary improved. In so doing, he lost her to the marchese, remained unmarried himself, and, though he served as governor of the island of San Diego, has been forced to retire to a lonely life and is about to lose his home.

Rolls feels he has been "possessed" throughout his life, that "it was difficult to tell what Rolls had been. Over him there was ruled a long straight honourable—and exceedingly efficient, in spite of its stultified end—straight line; perhaps they were right and it was red tape, a piece of good red tape called a career; pasted down over him. It hid him entirely." In a tone reminiscent of T. S. Eliot's Prufrock, he asks himself, "What was I? What did I do? Where was I?" (68).

Suddenly, with the appearance of Grizel, Rolls has an opportunity for renewal. He warns her that, as it did for him, the house will enter into her, forcing Grizel to lose some of her self-centeredness. For Grizel, this may not be a bad thing, for she is like and unlike her namesake, Griselda. Like Griselda in her independence, she has never yielded to anyone or anything. She will learn to do so as she acknowledges that she is "only human," a "hotchpotch" that includes many influences (73). One of these influences will come in the form of Pilot Officer Masterson, aptly called Pax, who is also an Italian marchese. It turns out he is Lark's nephew and knows the house intimately because of stories his aunt has told him about it. It was perhaps Pax's boyhood spirit or Pax's and Grizel's future son, Verity, that Rolls has sometimes seen flitting through the house.

For Pax wants a child. Proclaiming his faith in the future, he urges marriage on Grizel, who resists, wanting to maintain control over her own life. Much earlier, Griselda had questioned her doctor's faith in the ceaseless birth of children, saying, "How funny to be hopeful" (216). Dr. Flower responds, "I believe it will ultimately be just," a belief that, despite all the wasted lives in the house's history, seems reinforced by Pax's statement: a child is "only an act of faith . . . a link" (222). When Grizel doesn't seem to understand the importance of the house and marriage, Rolls quotes the lines from Eliot that preface the book: "Home is where one starts from . . ." (218). Moved by the power of poetry, the house, and the handsome Pax, Grizel achieves peace (in more ways than one), concurring that "all the new children ought to be links," that a child "would link us all up, link Lark and Rolls again through you and me" (223).

With this acknowledgment, the book moves toward its deus ex machina. The owner of the house agrees to a renewed lease. The house will go on in the hands of Grizel and Pax. Rolls, who has been holding internal monologues with Lark (who has, unknown to him, been dead for a month), gives Grizel the pearls Lark rejected years ago. He joins Lark in eternity when a bomb falls near the house, shattering the window on which Rolls rests his head but sparing the rest of the house.

It would seem that the house on Wiltshire Place absorbs the pain as well as the joy of its inhabitants. Selina's life shows the reverse side of self-sacrifice, naked bitterness and sadism. Rolls's life as an adult, too, is rife with disappointment. And Griselda's suffering in marriage and motherhood was intense. Her story permits her no redemption. It presents a picture of the grown woman's life as unbearable sacrifice, a picture that emerges in many of Godden's adult female characters. But there is reason for hope if the very long view is taken. The suffering of Griselda, Selina, and Rolls is somehow redeemed by Grizel and Pax's potential happiness, by the lessons Grizel and Pax may learn from the past, and by their unborn children, who may achieve yet more understanding and happiness. In Godden's vision, to be more fully explored from many perspectives, no one person's story is complete in itself.

The River

In *Take Three Tenses,* the imperfection of each individual life is somewhat mitigated by the interrelationship of all lives across the generations, facilitated by the house that has witnessed all the pains and triumphs of its occupants. Marriage is often seen as unsatisfactory, the unfulfilled woman limited in her ability to give love to her children. Yet, over the generations, the implication is that relationships improve even if, in Godden's novel, the woman still has to be persuaded it is her destiny to marry the man.

In *The River,* as in *Breakfast with the Nikolides,* childhood is seen as a brief interlude invaded by early glimpses of mortality or betrayal. The movement into experience is jagged, jarring, painful in the extreme, scarring the young girl who survives it. She is saved only by the intensity of her own will and by her determination to make the world her own through consciousness and poetry. In *Breakfast with the Nikolides* and *The*

River, both young girls learn that one ignores reality at one's peril; that true living and true art require constant attention; that all life, death, and art are one; and that these truths can be affirmed through ritual.

If in *Take Three Tenses* the lives of the people in the house on Wiltshire Place are interwoven across the generations, in Godden's next novel the implication is that life is a great river in which all people, despite differences, share in the same story. In *Breakfast with the Nikolides,* Godden had used the image of the river as a reflecting pool for Louise's past and present pain, as a vehicle for Emily's movement from innocence to experience, and as a mirror for the healing process that Emily undergoes through *puja. The River* begins with a description of the river in Bengal that is the book's setting, but Godden emphasizes that this could be a river anywhere. It is a universal water, and the drama enacted beside it is the eternal one of the passage from innocence to experience, birth to death, pain to healing. Although the eleven-year-old protagonist of the novel, Harriet, would like to stop this river of life and death and control it, she will learn in the course of the book that she cannot.

In *The River,* Bea, Harriet, Victoria, and their younger brother, Bogey, live with their mother and father, who supervises a jute-pressing works. Unlike the Godden children, who were sent back to England during the war, this foursome remain in India, but the war is much on their minds. Harriet initially feels uncomfortable with the fact of the war, embodied in Captain John, a young man who has been wounded, has escaped from a prisoner of war camp, and has an artificial leg. He will eventually teach Harriet important lessons about life and death and even, through her growing jealousy of his attraction to Bea, about love. Like the young Roly Dane, the children are being tutored in grammar—here, the Latin declensions of love and war. Like Roly, Harriet resists the more routinized facts of life, "Latin, and algebra and music . . . eating liver, having an injection."[3] Harriet especially resists the fact of death, which is omnipresent, not only in the far-off war but more immediately in India, in the ashes of the dead, for example, that the children see thrown into the river, and closer to home, when their pet guinea pig dies.

These occurrences exist as "cracks in the wholeness of Harriet's unconsciousness" (52) that move her inexorably toward an adulthood she tries to resist: "Now she was growing rapaciously." Struggling to understand how anyone integrates the reality of death, she listens to Bea talk about the "warm" part, going on to "something somewhere" (57), and to her mother talk about reincarnation. Harriet is also influenced by Captain John's ideas about the interpenetration of all life—"we go on being born

again and again because we have to, with each thing that happens to us, each new episode." "Growing," he tells Harriet, is "often painful and difficult" (44). Although Harriet is comforted, she believes that this growth is something that will take place later in her life. But soon she will reach a fuller understanding as she crosses the threshold of experience.

Harriet and Bea agree that life as an adult, punctuated as it is by love and war, seems less preferable than life as a child. "Half of Harriet wanted to stay as a child; half wanted to be a grown-up" (20). These oppositions are reflected in the images of birth and death, egg and snake. Sometimes Harriet feels enclosed in an egg like a chick waiting to be born but lacking a beak to break through; sometimes she meditates on the image of the snake and remembers her nanny's comment that we all change our skins seven times in our lives. The impulse toward growth and death implicit in this image of shedding skin is reminiscent of Captain John's comment that we die a little bit each time we grow (44).

In her dream of becoming a poet, Harriet takes refuge from the complex and often harsh realities of change, mortality, and the emptiness that adulthood seems to present—"so many grown-up people seem to be nothing very much" (21), she muses. When her nanny says everyone must grow up, "willy-nilly," Harriet dislikes the lack of choice the phrase implies, and when she vows to become a poet, parodies it, saying she will become a poet, "willy-nilly" (7). Becoming a writer is, in fact, anything but "willy-nilly" for Harriet. Envisioning one of her poems still extant in "say, A.D. 4000," Harriet vows to "work and work and work" (59) and be very "good," like Queen Victoria.

All the children have their private worlds. Harriet writes poems and deposits them in her secret hole in the jetty. The younger Victoria builds houses out of straw and rugs. Bogey is private and self-absorbed, and Bea is beginning to flirt with Captain John. Despite Harriet's wish to remain a child, she catches glimpses of experience, of Captain John helping Bea off a pony "as if she were a grown-up, not a child" (65), that begin to register faintly on her and make her frown.

But if Bea is growing up, and Harriet feels unconscious pangs of jealousy, Bogey resists growing up entirely, refusing to learn to read, insisting he won't be "any of those men" who "go to office" or "sign letters" (78). In fact, Bogey refuses to accept Christmas gifts, saying he "wants nothing." Someone with no wants, without desire, cannot survive in Godden's books. Bogey is destined to achieve his one wish, not to grow up. Indeed, it is an omen that when Nan drops pieces of lead into water to form charms that predict the future for the children, Bogey's piece

refuses to jell. Rather than become a model child, he dies. Harriet is in part to blame for his death because of her self-involvement and refusal to face facts. Although Bogey has told her he's been feeding a snake, she tells no one; he dies of a snakebite.

When Bogey is found dead under a tree, it is a shock to everyone, and the peace in the garden of Eden in which the children sometimes seem to live is shattered. Harriet is amazed that life continues as before. The knowledge of death has obsessed her throughout the book; now she must accept her implication in it and, by so doing, the human condition. When a young acquaintance discovers Harriet's journal and reads it aloud, revealing that Harriet knew there was a snake in the garden, Harriet can no longer claim she is innocent. She learns it is dangerous to be unthinking. She also learns that there are natural consequences, that art, though it can provide some measure of connection to others and to immortality, cannot evade the facts of life.

Still, Harriet comes to perceive her identity, to know that "this is me," when she witnesses the festival lights and to understand that while a bit of her has died with her brother, she is changing and growing. Though initially horrified at the thought, she learns that she can write about her own pain. That she is indeed a writer is evident in the deepening of her poetry. The earlier, clichéd poem—"The river runs, the round world spins" (7)—is replaced by her sense that "this tree, my tree is the pole of the world" (63). Everyone, she has come to understand, seeks his or her own pole, tree, or center. Bogey died under his tree, Captain John still seeks his, and Harriet has found hers in writing, which, despite her pain, will presumably offer her shelter and fruit throughout the coming years.

The Dolls' House

If the power of such imagery as the river, the house, the tree, and poetry itself (which draws on these images) can to some extent help children like Emily, Roly, and Harriet bind their pain and have faith in the future, the children in Godden's dolls' books find supportive images for their fears, hopes, and desires in the figure of the doll. In *Narratives of Love and Loss,* Margaret and Michael Rustin discuss, from a psychoanalytic perspective, how dolls can represent internal objects in the imagination of children and can and provide "intense and moving symbolizations of [their] emotional preoccupations."[4]

In *The Dolls' House,* Godden's first book with doll protagonists, the Rustins see the conflict between sensitive Charlotte and her more action-

oriented sister, Emily, reflected in the tension between two dolls, the affectionate and loyal Tottie and the grandiose and untouchable Marchpane. Marchpane is ultimately relegated to a museum that for the Rustins represents "the archaic area of the self which houses those primitive elements of emotionality which have been outgrown in the course of development" (88). This triumph over grandiosity symbolizes the real girls' emotional growth.

The subject matter of *The Dolls' House* is very much like that of *The River,* published the previous year, revolving as it does around a death in the family and the wish for continuity. The theme that all is one, so central to *Breakfast with the Nikolides, Take Three Tenses,* and *The River,* is at the heart of *The Dolls' House.* Tottie Plantagenet is the small Dutch doll who has lived in the Dane nursery for many generations, belonging now to Emily and Charlotte Dane, but to their great-grandmother and great-great-aunt before them as well (the name Dane is reminiscent of the family name in *Take Three Tenses,* as is the theme of continuity). Tottie is made of "good wood" and sometimes still feels the strength of "the sap that ran through it and made it bud and put out leaves every spring and summer, that kept it strong through the winter storms and wind." Tottie says to herself, "a little, a very little of that tree is in me."[5]

In her essay "The Writer Must Become as a Child," Godden observes that in writing for children it is necessary to develop and maintain a child's perspective as well as an adult's, to "get down to a child's horizon." The best children's books of the past, Godden asserts, do not "have a big plot written down, but a little plot written up." Their writers were "within the child's horizon and knew that in it little things become big."[6]

In *The Dolls' House,* Godden views the world not only from the perspective of the child but from the microperspective of the doll. In this world, dolls come to life and are both similar to and different from the children who possess them and whom they possess. "It is an anxious, sometimes a dangerous thing to be a doll. Dolls cannot choose; they can only be chosen" (13). Dolls are perceived as powerless and passive, much as many adults perceive children. But if dolls do not seem to grow either emotionally or physically, and if this absence of growing pains may, in Godden's fictional world, make life easier for dolls than for children, it also means that their existence is subject to an eternity of control by others. Like the child protagonists in Godden's books, however, dolls have an important hidden ability to wish. They "cannot tell anything, but often their wish is as strong as telling. Have you never felt a doll's wish?" the author asks her readers (31).

No less than in her adult fiction, in Godden's children's books wishes structure reality. Tottie, an old-fashioned doll, lives with a motley makeshift family appointed by Emily and Charlotte. There is Mr. Plantagenet, a worn-out China doll with a drawn mustache who has been cast about and abused. Mrs. Plantagenet, or Birdie, who is made of celluloid and was once part of a Christmas decoration, is "not quite right in the head" (15), which rattles and reminds us of several unstable mother figures in Godden's fiction. There are also Apple, Tottie's brother, made of fabric; and Darner, the family dog, made of pipe cleaners.

As in much of Godden's fiction, despite their good intentions, Mr. and Mrs. Plantagenet are less than satisfactory parents. Their children end up caring for them rather than the reverse: "Really you might have thought that Tottie was the father and he was the child; but there are real fathers like that" (15). Nevertheless, the family is happy, only missing, as many Godden characters do, a home. When the children inherit an old wooden dolls' house that has been in the family for a very long time (Tottie once lived in it), the dolls, urged by Tottie, wish very hard for the Danes to keep it, clean it, and give it to them to live in and furnish with beds, chairs, couch, lace, and curtains. You must wish "over and over again," she tells them. "You must never leave off wishing" (42). And indeed, their wishes are all fulfilled.

But just as the doll family has settled into the house, Emily agrees to lend Tottie to a doll exhibition. Tottie thinks she's been sold because Emily receives money for the loan, and, separated from her doll family, she feels orphaned. At the exhibit, she encounters Marchpane, an elegant doll with a haughty disposition (she dislikes children) who is also owned by the Danes and who had lived in the wooden dolls' house several generations ago. While Tottie's sap rises in pleasure when she learns she has not been sold, it sinks again when she realizes Marchpane will be coming home with her. Marchpane takes over the household, relegating the Plantagenet parents to the role of maid and butler and claiming Apple (who is attracted by the superficial Marchpane) as her son.

Birdie Plantagenet performs the ultimate sacrifice when Apple, neglected by Marchpane, almost falls into the fire. She pulls herself together and throws herself between Apple and the lamp. Emily and Charlotte, who have been charmed by Marchpane's beauty, are now repelled, for they notice that Marchpane alone made no move toward Apple in his distress. All of the other dolls moved minutely; indeed, as Godden remarks in an interview, as a child, she was "quite convinced" that dolls "would move if I wasn't looking at them."[7]

Marchpane is consigned to a museum where she is much happier untouched, and the house is restored to the Plantagenets. Tottie learns that "things come and things pass. . . . Everything from trees to dolls. . . . Even for small things like us, even for dolls" (135). Interestingly, at the end of the book, Tottie still seems to be protecting Mr. Plantagenet. When Mr. Plantagenet asks Tottie, "But the good things have come back, haven't they?" Tottie answers, "'Of course they have'. . . in her kind wooden voice" (136), and there is a sense that Birdie's spirit continues to live in the house.

Emily, the central human character in *The Dolls' House,* is like Tottie in her creative ideas and strong will. In the course of the story she learns to be a better mother to her dolls, to modify her wishes with thought so as not to make mistakes (such as preferring Marchpane or accepting money for lending Tottie to the exhibition). Unlike the children in *Breakfast with the Nikolides* or *The River,* however, she suffers no profound loss. In *The Dolls' House,* unlike *The River,* a brother is rescued, albeit at the expense of the mother. If death is three-dimensional and center stage in *The River,* it is in *The Dolls' House* held at arm's length and reduced to doll-sized proportions. Indeed, as Godden comments in an interview, *The Dolls' House* is really a murder mystery, although only John Betjeman realized it (Wintle and Fisher, 291). Is Birdie then murdered by Marchpane's wishes? Is the good mother murdered by the bad, and does this loss of maternal care enable Tottie to come into her own in the home? It is perhaps not surprising that an emotionally exhausting book such as *The River* was followed shortly by one in which wishes triumph and death's sting is reduced to celluloid, whatever the story's more serious implications.

A Candle for St. Jude

A Candle for St. Jude, like *The River,* is concerned with finding one's own "tree" or center through art, here the art of ballet. The story, rambling and with wooden characters, focuses on the consciousness of an adult, with the child character peripheral. It is of interest primarily as it foreshadows two later novels that revolve around ballet and child dancers, *Thursday's Children* (1984) and *Listen to the Nightingale* (1992), to be discussed later.

In *A Candle for St. Jude,* Madame Anna Holbein, whom Godden has referred to as "almost a 'stock figure'" (Simpson, 52), has been head of a ballet school and theater in London for thirty years. She is a self-centered, jealous woman who feels taken for granted and keeps relics of her brilliant dancing past in a cabinet on the stairs. In her old country, Russia, Madame was known as Niura. She often remembers someone who loved her saying, "Listen, Niura, that is a nightingale."[8] Although she cannot recall who said it or what it meant, she does remember becoming "Anna" when her older brother took the orphaned girl to St. Petersburg and she began her training for the ballet. While Madame Holbein has lost touch with the Niura of her childhood—"could not remember her at all" (132)—she is interested in one of her pupils, named Lollie, who "seemed to her a reflection of herself" (63). Although Madame feels sympathy for all "lost children," for those who are "lost in the immensity of the world they had to fight" and who "seemed to have no strength to borrow from but hers" (63), she has a realistic view and does not "make excuses for them either as people or dancers" (65). She looks at her pupils as "eggs" because "we don't know what they will hatch into" (65). She both taunts and encourages Lollie, saying, "Perhaps you would rather be a dressmaker, say, like your aunt?" When Lollie hesitates to audition for a role as a dancer in a new film, she tells her, "Your horizon is no bigger than this saucer" (62) and must expand. "You believe you are going to be a dancer. Already you have to do for that, things that other children don't do . . . you must suffer for it" (64).

Lollie will, of course, pass the audition and come to the forefront in the similar character of Lottie in Godden's later book *Listen to the Nightingale* (1992). In *A Candle for St. Jude,* however, her story is inter-mixed with that of Hilda, a seventeen-year-old dancer whom Madame distrusts: Hilda was "a snake . . . or something to do with a snake . . . is it Eve?" (38). Madame is jealous of Hilda's talent, which she describes as "too strong" (39), and prefers the milder, lamblike Caroline. Although Hilda has "very white skin," she reminds Madame Holbein not only of a snake and of Eve but also of an "Egyptian" (38)—which for the elderly ballet-mistress connotes a Gypsy. As Madame Holbein remarks to the musician Mr. Felix, "Egyptian is another name for gypsy" (21). Indeed, Godden's fascination with the image of the Gypsy or dark-skinned, dark-haired waif figure of mysterious origin will manifest itself in numer-ous works. These isolated, romantic figures are filled with a creative energy that will ultimately enable them to triumph as a result of willpower and the help of supporting figures.

Hilda feels depleted, unable to make a mark on the world despite her great talents as a choreographer; she cannot accept Madame's wish to change her ballet in any way. She feels cut off from the past and is convinced that it is more difficult to make a mark in the present than in Madame's time. Hilda's complement, Lollie, possesses the restraint Hilda lacks, and the reader senses that she will realize her potential in the future. When Hilda complains of feeling like a "pinprick," Lollie responds, "Well, we are a star as well" (121).

In the end, Hilda will get the recognition she needs, Madame acknowledging Hilda's superiority to Caroline when her protégé's faults become too obvious and when Hilda flawlessly dances the role in a ballet in which Madame once herself starred. Hilda will, through yielding to the needs of the company, learn that a connection to the past and others is important, too. Madame Holbein will recognize that it is time for her to give credit where it is due to Hilda and that it is essential to "bring together the component parts" (155). She must accept that the dancer Lion loves Hilda, not her, that Mr. Felix has been right in saying "you don't hear music as music anymore," and that she has preferred the "conventional, the pretty, the traditional" and been myopic in seeing Caroline as the star (19). Now, with Hilda's production and Lollie's audition successful, the school's sinking reputation has been saved. Was it by the candle her sister-in-law Ilse lit for St. Jude, patron of lost causes, or by Madame's own ability to bring the component parts together?

It will take forty years before Godden publishes another book on the theme of ballet, but when she does, the component parts of what she only sketchily describes in *A Candle for St. Jude* will emerge in a much more focused light.

One may view the books of the 1940s, in which children hold center stage, against the backdrop of two books written a few years earlier, in which the child's role is peripheral. The narrator in *Chinese Puzzle* (1936) has lived a selfish, manipulative life and attributes his loss of humanity and transformation into a Pekingese dog to his failure to produce children: "I gave way to my Desires, caring nothing that I left no Son to keep my spirit for me."[9] He feels that children are not "terribly interesting" and that humans tend their young too long. When at last he sires some pups, he dies, feeling released. He leaves the manuscript of his life's story for a furry friend to unearth after his passing. Here, children are seen as an uninteresting but fundamental duty. Once this duty has been fulfilled, the parent may be able to meet his or her own needs or even, if too tired, have the luxury of dying, preferably after having produced an immortal work of art. Does this book, completed about the time Godden's first daughter, Jane, was born in 1935, reveal some of Godden's personal early ambivalence about the sometimes opposing demands of motherhood and art?

Gypsy, Gypsy (1940) is intriguing in what it hints about eighteen-year-old Henrietta's childhood with her Aunt Barbe. Spellbound by Barbe, whose sharp character matches her name, Henrietta has been unable to leave her. As she explains, "What guts I had were taken out of me when I was about fourteen."[10] Was Henrietta a victim of molestation at the hands of Barbe's gentleman callers—"She never bothered to hide things from me . . . I was only a child, and even a child was game" (13–14)— or was she corrupted by Barbe herself? Needless to say, this undercurrent is unexplored, but it will reemerge overtly fifty-four years later in Godden's most recent work, *Pippa Passes* (1994). Henrietta's fiancé, René, says of Barbe, "I've heard that some poor creatures think to cure themselves of disease by intercourse with a wretched child—it's vile but understandable," but it is "to destroy a soul . . ." (114). In any case, as a child, Henrietta was warned by Barbe not to "confide in anyone," and, indeed, when she tries to talk about her terrible secret at school, the teachers send her away; as Barbe explains, "They're afraid you'll lead the lambs astray" (114–15).

In these two books, in which childhood is glimpsed offstage, children are seen as necessary burdens or as paralyzed victims of others' malevolence. The vision of childhood is darkened as children exist only in the shadows of adults, having few resources with which to assert their integrity.

Chapter Three

Rootedness versus Chaos, 1951–1958

On the whole, Godden's children's books permit the child more potential fulfillment of wishes and desires, more possibility to develop and make use of the resources of the self than do her novels for adults. For Godden, children's books have their own ethic, which, while not requiring authors to condescend to the child, does require that evil not triumph. Furthermore, as the previous chapter notes, Godden's adult books with child protagonists seem, at least through the 1940s, to allow the child more importance and self-determination than those in which the child figure is peripheral.

Indeed, the very act of addressing the child as audience in a children's book, or focusing on the child figure in adult fiction, is to a degree an affirmation, a statement of value and hopefulness. It is, after all, a symptom of adult unease if the child's potential is portrayed as limited or paralyzed. What then of works for children in which the protagonists are mice, and the subject matter the role of the mother in relation to her husband and children? While *The Mousewife* and *Mouse House* fall into the range of other animal tales of the 1940s and 1950s, like E. B. White's *Stuart Little* and *Charlotte's Web,* they show the dark aspect of the adult woman's family life: how life in the household of the family can shadow her life in the house of the self. The mothers in *The Mousewife* and *Mouse House* share the conflicts of Sophie, the mother in *Kingfishers Catch Fire*—all are torn between rootedness and possible chaos, between caring for their families and taking flight. In *Mouse House* and *Kingfishers Catch Fire,* as in *An Episode of Sparrows* and *The Greengage Summer* (where the stories are written from the children's perspectives), mothers are preoccupied with their own problems, leaving their children to explore the tension between rootedness and chaos on their own, sometimes to find in the process their own homes or transformed selves.

The Mousewife

The theme of the restless woman trapped by husband and family that runs through many of Godden's books for adults is adumbrated in *The Mousewife* (1951), a story inspired by an anecdote in Dorothy Wordsworth's *Journal* about a mouse and a caged dove. In a note to *The Mousewife*, Godden remarks that unlike Dorothy Wordsworth, who fails to free the dove at the end, she feels it important that her own mousewife do so.

In the Godden story, all the house mice in Miss Wilkinson's comfortable old home are happy except for the Mousewife, who, while outwardly resembling the others, wishes for more, and cannot answer her husband's question, "What more do you want?" His, "Why don't you think about cheese?" fails to engage her response, and while his wife takes good care of him, their relationship is a tepid one. When her husband falls ill, the Mousewife (like Rumer Godden when Laurence left) is burdened with finding food for the entire family. "She had no time for thinking."[1]

But at this time, as in Dorothy Wordsworth's tale, a caged dove is brought home to the house where the mice live, so sad it refuses to eat. The Mousewife decides to take some of the bird's food for her family, but she is frightened away when the listless bird moves. She visits the dove and urges him to eat and drink, but, like Kafka's Hunger Artist, the dove cannot eat ordinary food and drinks "only dew," the liquid of the free. In their conversations, the Mousewife's education about freedom begins: "What is fly?" the Mousewife asks. "Don't you know?" the surprised dove replies, and tries to demonstrate, but the cage is too small (14).

Her husband wonders why the Mousewife spends so much time on the windowsill; he says, "The proper place for a mousewife is in her hole or coming out for crumbs and frolic with me" (16). Soon, like Griselda in *Take Three Tenses*, the Mousewife has a new brood of babies to keep her busy. The dove is neglected, and when the Mousewife finally visits him, he is sorely drooping. "'I thought you had gone, gone, gone,' he said over and over again" (19). The Mousewife spends a long time with the dove, and her husband responds to her unexplained absence with abuse. "When she went home," writes Godden, "I am sorry to say, her husband bit her on the ear" (20).

In bed that night, the Mousewife finds time to think, and decides it is "thoughtless of Miss Barbara Wilkinson" to keep the dove in a cage. "'To sit in the trap until your little bones are stiff and your whiskers grow stupid because there is nothing for them to smell or hear or see!' The mousewife could only think of it as a mouse, but she could feel as the dove could feel" (20–22).

Quietly scampering to the dove's cage, she opens the catch and he escapes, taking her breath away with him at the beauty of his flight— "'So that is to fly,' she said, 'Now I know'" (25). As she perches on the window, the Mousewife sees the stars only described to her by the dove and knows she is changed—"without the dove. I can see for myself" (28). The Mousewife lives to be a very old and well-respected great-great-grandmother, and she retains the knowledge that though she looks like all other mice, "she is a little different from them" (30).

Mouse House

In Rumer Godden's hierarchy, mice live on a level different from that of dolls. Like dolls, mice appear to be unchanged throughout the generations. As Godden comments in *The Mousewife*, "If a mouse could have a portrait painted of his great great grandfather, and his great grandfather, it would be the portrait of a mouse today" (4). But despite their apparent lack of evolution and inability to affect humans through their wishes (as can dolls), mice (unlike dolls) do have the ability to move, which gives them a vitality that can represent the life force itself.

In *Mouse House*, little Mary's father gives her a red painted dolls' house with two toy mice, fancy furniture, and wallpaper, in which to keep her jewelry. But Mary is more taken with the real mice in the cellar, who seem to represent the true hidden life in the story, stirring about in the depths of the house of the self. In this mouse-world, father mouse scolds mother mouse for having so many children and takes no responsibility for them. The mouse children sleep in a tumble in a flower pot, and the youngest, Bonnie, is pushed on the floor. When, suffering from low self-esteem—"Nobody wants me"—Bonnie seeks refuge in the dolls' house, its door locks behind her, causing her to panic. "Have you ever been shut in? Then you will know how it feels. . . . "Let me out! Let me out!' "[2] Bonnie cries. These words, echoing the feelings of many of Godden's female characters, are surely meant on more than one level; they are a desperate cry for the full expression of the self.

Mother mouse misses her youngest, but her husband denies a child is missing and speaks derisively to his wife. "*You* can't count" (38), he says. When his wife asks him to find a better house for the family, he replies, "What, *me*?" and "I'm eating." For the mice of this world, consumption is the only good. In fact, not only won't the mouse-man provide, but he puts the burden on the children: "The houth ith for the children," he retorts, his mouth full, "Leth the children look" (40).

Indeed, Bonnie does join the category of children who fend for themselves and their families. When Bonnie messes up the dolls' house, Mary puts it in the cellar, where the other mice take it apart and make it into the family home. They give Bonnie its bed as a sort of house-finder's fee, and, as Mother Mouse says, so that "she can never be pushed out again." As Bonnie says, however, "If I hadn't been pushed out . . . we shouldn't have Mousehouse" (61)—or, one might add, the initiative, selfhood, and community that the Mousehouse represents. Like Hansel and Gretel and others who have been pushed out of their homes and forced to draw on their own resources, she managed in so doing to find strength.

Mary, whose story figures as a frame for the mouse tale, ends up giving the toy mice, tied to a pincushion, to her aunt. She is a child who has little tolerance for falsehood, and feels that the real mice are part of her: "They are *my* mice . . . I gave them Mousehouse" (63), she observes. The point seems to be that the self, though sometimes chaotic and scrambling, will ultimately seek its own house. The story also touches on a question underlying other Godden fiction: is it in fact necessary for children to be somewhat (or even seriously) neglected if they are to find their true selves?

Kingfishers Catch Fire

If the mythical Greek kingfisher, Alcyone, drowned herself to join her husband in death, Sophie, heroine of *Kingfishers Catch Fire* (1953), finds in her husband's absence and then death an opportunity to plunge deeply into the waters of the self in search of happiness, the "halcyon days" the compassionate gods bestowed on the kingfisher's breeding place. In so doing, she puts not only herself but her two children at extreme risk. Yet like the kingfishers, who "when they plunged for a fish and opened their wings and flew there was a flash of colour and they glowed,"[3] Sophie, in Gerard Manley Hopkins's words in his poem "As Kingfishers Catch Fire," is able to "catch fire" and arise from the depths, as much phoenix as kingfisher.

The book begins with a short preface postdating the conclusion by two years. Sophie's friend Toby gives her "another lamp with kingfishers on it" from Kashmir. The significance of this gift, and of his understanding that Sophie herself is "like a kingfisher herself, choosing some strange unthought-of place for her nest, diving relentlessly for her private fish, then flashing out of sight" (2), isn't evident till the end of the story itself. The ambiguous nature of Sophie's promise that she will not lose this lamp as she lost the first—"I am more careful now"—and her casual comment that she is "homesick" for Kashmir will also be suggested as the story unfolds. For in the course of both the recorded story and the unwritten pages between the conclusion and the preface, much has happened to transform Sophie (and Toby), and, one hopes, much will continue to be inscribed in their lives, whether they remain together or apart.

Independent of mind, restless, thirty-five-year-old Sophie has at the beginning of the story left her handsome but weak husband Denzil at a remote Indian post to roam Kashmir with her two children. Denzil dies from a cold, and Sophie finally decides to lease the idyllic but run-down villa, Dhilkusha, and its gardens in Kashmir for five years. Then, having rendered herself nearly penniless by repaying Denzil's debts after his death, she determines to live like a peasant. She wishes to survive independently, to seize the opportunity to redefine her life and her children's and to make the meaning of the house's name, "to make the heart glad," a reality for all of them.

Early on, she notices a star-like cross cut into the verandah floor and learns it was made by an unknown Gypsy sailor passing through. This becomes a symbol of Sophie's wanderlust and is contrasted with her distaste for limits, for those "edges, pressing against each other, hurting, jarring, offending, barring one human being from another, shutting away their understanding and their souls" (65); yet, Sophie recognizes, "if you have no edges . . . how lonely, how drifting, you must consent to be." The thrust of this book is toward balance, toward finding that delicate line between movement and stasis, drifting and anchorage, chaos and place that constitutes life.

Sophie's aunts in England have warned her that she has not learned the law of cause and effect and that one day "she will be punished" and others will be hurt as well (7). Her own daughter, Teresa, agrees. The antithesis of Sophie, Teresa is a stolid, realistic, rooted being; at eight years old, she seems caught between childhood and early adulthood. Fearful when Sophie gets restless because she knows she and her few possessions will be uprooted again, Teresa is chastised by Sophie as slow and timid, a "little nuisance" (30). Despite Sophie's love for her and wish to make her happy, Teresa is in some ways a surly and neglected child. It is she who must care for her young brother, "Moo," when Sophie works all day at Dhilkusha to provide the children with everything she thinks they need and, in so doing, contracts typhoid. When Teresa anxiously calls to the dangerously ill Sophie, Sophie feels, "I am deaf . . . I am gone . . . I can't," and thinks, "Teresa always was a tiresome child" (30). Brought up on Sophie's exotic ideas (Sophie dismisses English children as too proper and boring and insists that Teresa immediately accept the herdschildren at Dhilkusha as her brothers and sisters), Teresa is poignantly grateful for simple facts such as information about Sophie's health. Certain, even when Sophie recovers, that her mother cannot take care of her children adequately, Teresa yearns for the safety of her old row house in Camberley, England, where "we had a gate" (75).

Sensitive but accepting of their many moves, Moo is also neglected, although he has a surrogate mother in Teresa. When Sophie ties his hands behind his back because he persists in cutting flowers, it is Teresa who screams at her that she is a cruel, wicked mother. Sophie's unusual attempt to establish limits has been overly harsh. Moo falls into the water and, nearly drowning, is rescued by the herdschildren. While the children befriend Moo, they fight over him, almost killing him in the process, and thus bring into question one of Sophie's pet ideas about human nature—that it is innately good.

Teresa has been fearful of the herdschildren all along and also aware of the threat they pose to Sophie's ideas. Sophie has always "impressed on Teresa that she must think. '*Think* of other people. . . . *Think* what you are doing'" (151). Yet it is because Teresa "thinks" that she is slow and so is scolded by Sophie, who is herself quick and, most often, thoughtless of consequences. The herdschildren represent the life of impulse and the unconscious that Sophie professes to oppose. One day, the herdschildren fight over possession of Moo, and Teresa, stepping into the fray, is badly beaten. Hidden away in a cave by Sophie's servant Nabir, who fears that he will be accused of the crime, Teresa is discovered unconscious much later. She eventually recovers, but the fact that she was in such jeopardy is instrumental in helping Sophie reevaluate the effect of her thought-lessness on others.

Increasingly, Sophie will be forced to confront a radical discrepancy not only between her idealized view of childhood and reality but also between an idealized view of nature and art and reality. Children are not always carefree, as Sophie expects, nor are they always at one with nature; some-times they destroy nature. Neither is nature always supportive of human need. "People shouldn't die now. . . . It's Spring," Sophie laments (127), noting a disturbing disjunction in her view of the order of things.

Sophie's fixed ideas lead her to serious error when she disregards cus-tom and possible consequences and tries to befriend warring groups of

peasants. She sets up an herb garden to heal sick neighbors (taking business away from the local "doctor"-barber), which leads to grave repercussions. Herbs should heal, not harm, but she will learn they can harm
toward the end of the book when the barber encourages Sophie's servant
Sultan to control her with a deadly "love potion." Soon the peaceful garden is transformed into what the children call "the Quarrelling place,"
because, as Teresa explains to Sophie, "it's used for quarrelling" (131) by
the servants, neighbors, and children. Sophie longs for peace and for
healing, which, as the missionary Dr. Glenister explains to Teresa, means
"to make whole" (77). In Sophie's idealized view of childhood, division,
anger, and quarrelling are unacceptable. Children, she tells Teresa,
should not argue but write poems (as suggested by a book Sophie purchases called *The Wise Teacher*). But when Teresa writes a poem, it is
about quarrelling. Unable to live up to Sophie's prescription that a
"child should be happy and confident" (131), Teresa soon stops commu-
nicating altogether.

Sophie chooses the aesthetic, her vision of the ideal, over the reality of
the Kashmirian world and her own children. She tries to forge
Dhilkhusha into an orderly work of art against the backdrop of poverty
and death in which the skeletons of children are washed up daily by the
river. Using money meant to take the children on a camping trip, she
purchases from Profit David the merchant an expensive Kirman rug, the
splendor of which fills her soul. As the savvy merchant tells her, "You are
an artist, Lady Sahib. You have been starving your soul" (179).

When Teresa learns the money is gone, she is profoundly disappointed at the broken promise of escape from the summer heat. "We don't
keep things," she cries (180), not accepting art as a substitute for life. In
contrast, for Teresa, the only valued objects are the few ordinary ones of
daily life she has been able to salvage from move to move, such as her
favorite doll and a blue and white teapot. Like the facts Teresa prefers to
ideas, these things represent security and serve as magic objects offering
a link from past to future. Indeed, although as her Aunt Rose will later
say, at Dhilkhusha Sophie tried to create a place of purity and peace, and
although even Teresa in time comes to feel at home there, the house will
soon turn against them all.

Ongoing conflicts and misunderstandings between Sophie and others
signal Sophie's alienation from her environment but are also sympto-
matic of the difficulty of communication in a universe in which all language is deconstructed, its multiple meanings dependent on one's
perspective. In her essay "On Words," Godden conjectures, if "books

were Persian carpets, one would assess their value through minute examination of stitching as well as pattern," for "the stitch of a book is its
words," which have "shades and shades of meaning—and countless
shades of sound."[4] In *Kingfishers Catch Fire,* Godden repeatedly examines
the stitching of language itself, defining and redefining words as if to
bridge gaps in communication and to bring about healing. There seems
to be agreement about the definition of Dhilkhusha ("to make glad")
and of "healing" ("to make whole"). But various meanings are attributed
to other words and phrases that point to different worldviews. For
Sophie, a "good missionary" is one who accepts Kashmiris as her brothers, even sharing their dirty bread. Teresa, on the other hand, expresses
dismay at the peasants' dirtiness, yet she wants to be a missionary; she is
confused and pained by her mother's ironic remark, "You will make a
good missionary when you grow up" (78–79). Similarly, for Sophie, a
"peasant" is the image of an ideal, a romanticized haze of a natural man;
for the children's Kashmiri nurse, it is a term of contempt. And when
Sophie tries to persuade Teresa that reading is a shared bond between
mother and child and quotes the Bible, "My peace I give unto you,"
Teresa asks, "Piece of what?" (95)

At the heart of the book is the word "love"—a word that has suffered
many interpretations throughout the ages. When the servant Sultan,
soon to cause much trouble, asks Sophie for money to buy a watch or
bicycle and is rejected, he says, "the Memsahib doesn't love me," and
Sophie replies, "Love is a very big word." Even as she says this, she feels
compassion for Sultan, but for him love means only money (112). In her
attempt to be generous, Sophie gives the peasants many gifts. "What I
give, I give without stint," she says, but when the meaning of the word
"stint" is explained to Profit David, he says, "I like stint," and when she
comments, "Nothing venture, nothing win," he thinks "'venture' a terrible word" (142). Sophie consistently gives words a spiritual value,
ignoring the material perspective; this is, as she will soon discover, to her
peril.

Misused language leads to the edge of tragedy, but it also helps effect
Sophie's transformation. Sultan, who is secretly in love with Sophie, asks
her for a recipe for a "love-potion" for someone. Reading from her old-
fashioned book of herbs, Sophie mentions, among other ingredients, dissolved pearls. Over the next weeks, Teresa (who is observant of facts),
notices her food is gritty. Sophie becomes increasingly lethargic, sexually
aroused, and ill. When tests are done, it is discovered that she has been
given charras, or Indian hemp (marijuana), which can induce hallucina-

tions, and that ground glass has been put in her food. Although the guilty Sultan and the innocent Nabir (he is suspected of harming Teresa in the incident with the herdschildren) are arrested, Sophie comes to feel that Nabir is not guilty and that even in the case of Sultan there has been a misunderstanding.

After recovering sufficiently, Sophie goes to visit Sultan and discovers that he meant to give her a "love drink" to bend her will to his. The ground glass is his interpretation of dissolved pearls: "Glass is imitation jewels. You said jewels" (241). Sophie, now on a quest for facts, returns to Dhilkhusha. Questioning a herdschild, she discovers that it was the children who hurt Teresa, not Nabir. Her new determination to confront reality impels her to force the authorities to release Nabir.

Indeed, as Sophie believes, the potion (symbolic of her entire experience at Dhilkusha) has worked: "I am loving . . . they have had their way. I love these people and this place" (271), she tells Toby, her longtime friend and suitor, who has arrived deus ex machina from England (Teresa mails Toby a letter Sophie, in a weak moment when sick, has scribbled to him). Stolid and reliable, Toby is wholly unaware of what has happened around and inside Sophie: "These people have got hold of you," said Toby (269). "I know," Sophie replies, with different meaning. Although Sophie now feels able to live at Dhilkhusha again, on respectful terms with the villagers, the landlord has canceled her lease. Ironically, she is forced to move on when she would like stability—"she felt as if the sailor were ruthless, with his uncaring stars" (270).

But Sophie is now indeed at a crossroad. She must decide whether to return to England with Teresa as Toby's wife or to accept an offer to teach in Lebanon. In her refusal to permit Toby to pay Profit David what is still owed on her precious Kirman rug (symbolic of the world of art), she holds onto her faith in herself and her love of beauty, awaiting some "word" that will guide her. The word finally arrives, literally, in the form of a letter from Sophie's Aunt Rose, who sends money to "buy something of beauty for yourself out of this place you love" (277). The £100 will buy the little coral Chinese goddess of children, a statue that the merchant has loaned her.

Despite his materialistic name, for Sophie, Profit David represents the world of art and spirit (the prophetic). For Profit David, Sophie is like the emperors, who "suffered many things . . . and their children were always suffering too" (236–37). Although Sophie firmly rejects this elitist view of childhood suffering and sees Profit David as the effective salesman he is, in Godden's work children very often do suffer for the actions of adults who consider themselves special and lordly in some fashion. Sophie would never consciously allow her children to suffer and urges Teresa to return to England to live with her aunts, something Teresa, in a reversal of her previous stance, refuses to do. Teresa now wishes to stay with Sophie and Moo. She is disenchanted with Toby, who is trying to mold Moo into a "Thomas," a stereotypical English boy. In a complex strand running through her work, one senses Godden's conflict, expressed most strongly in her female characters, about whether experience gained by adults and children as a result of a mother's "ventures" is worth the uncalculated price of the suffering extracted—mostly from children.

Aunt Rose's letter advises Sophie not to marry Toby: "Don't do it," the letter says—this from an actress aunt who always has advised that ideas must be tempered with discretion. Yet it was she who so long ago broke one stereotype by sending Moo a leaded doll, one that bounces back when pushed down. This doll, the prototype of which was sent to Godden by her sister Jon when Godden was four years old, is a recurrent image of resilience in Godden's work, an image that Eleanor Cameron sees also as a symbol of Godden's unswerving will to write.[5] When Toby fires Nabir because he thinks the servant's presence will disturb Sophie, Sophie takes action. One morning, while Toby sleeps, Sophie, Teresa, and Moo gather their belongings and gifts and head toward Lebanon, Sophie stopping only to talk to herself—"'The sailor is better for you' said Sophie to Sophie. 'Even if he is cold comfort, even if you never see him or catch his star. Take him for yours,'" and "Sophie said, 'I will,'" thus secretly "wedding" herself (282). Toby is last seen sleeping, the kingfishers glinting in the sun nearby.

Sophie has chosen to follow her own star, with her children, free of mortal man. She has learned some respect for the world of facts, including the fact that she needs to move on. And the children? Moo and Teresa have survived; Teresa seems somewhat changed, unwilling to choose the safety of England. Is it Sophie's illusion that the children will be all right? Have their experiences made the dangers worthwhile in the end? Is Sophie, on the other hand, still denying their needs, still permitting them to suffer for her growth? It is impossible to tell, although the reader is gratified that Sophie is no mousewife. When, two years later, she reappears with Toby in England, we see a change on both sides. Toby, who once had contempt for spending money on beautiful objects, has purchased a new kingfisher lamp to replace the one that's been lost. If he is more understanding, Sophie appears more careful. Yet she is homesick for Kashmir, and it is not at all clear what she will do next.

Kingfishers Catch Fire was written from the perspective of the adult and focuses on how a mother's struggle for independence can affect her children. It raises questions about whether any suffering children endure as a result of their parents' wants and adventures can be justified, whether the experience gained by adults and children can redeem the latter's painful loss of innocence. *An Episode of Sparrows* and *The Greengage Summer,* the next Godden novels, on the other hand, are written from the child's viewpoint. In these novels, children, this time in European settings, are, in one way or another, effectively abandoned by parents who figure in the most peripheral manner in the stories. Both novels explore what neglected children can accomplish on their own and what internal and external resources may be available to them. In so doing, they attack the question of the price of childhood experience and suffering from a perspective somewhat different from that of *Kingfishers Catch Fire.*

An Episode of Sparrows

An Episode of Sparrows (1955) derives its name from the children who play on Catford Street, the poor street that runs behind the imposing Mortimer Square. As Angela Chesney looks down (in both senses) on these children from the height of her grand house on the square, she sees them as "cheeky, cocky, common as sparrows." For her more sensitive sister, Olivia, they are also sparrows, but, as Godden often reminds us, "when two people say the same word, it can mean two different things." To Olivia, "nothing was common" in the sense of "vulgar"; Olivia rather muses over the biblical saying that "not one [Sparrow] should fall to the ground"[6]—the meaning of which will be strikingly revealed to her before the end of the novel.

The younger Angela had been raised as the golden child, with fair looks and prospects, given a larger inheritance, and trained as an accountant (their mother believed in educating girls). Now forty-five and unmarried, like her older sister, Angela, as her name suggests, is involved in good works. But if she is an angel, it is one who, ironically, lacks true compassion. Looking into the square, she notices holes where earth is missing and determines to track down and punish the children who have stolen it. Olivia, on the other hand, "born inept and clumsy" (11), untrained in worldly pursuits and uninterested in organized good works, retains a childlike ability to see into the true nature of things. She imagines the "earth tilting, slowly tilting, as it turned on its axis in the sky" and marvels that she, "a pinprick" in a "pinprick city can feel the

power of the earth" (12). She is intrigued not by the missing patches of
earth in the garden, but by the footprints in the garden bed. Who are
the children persistent enough to remove the earth in secret? What were
they doing? "What did they want?" she wonders. The word "want"
becomes a fulcrum for Olivia's musings about her own lost youth and
unfulfilled wants. She feels like Robinson Crusoe tracking Friday's footprints to an unspoiled Wordsworthian world in which children seem
"truer than grownups, unalloyed," "rooted in the earth, not in man-
made things." With children, she thinks, "you would be alive," with
"one real chance . . . to join in something real" (13–15). Throughout
much of the story, the sisters' lives will not directly coincide with the
children's, but by the end of the novel, the stories of the Chesneys and
the "sparrows" will intersect and Olivia's prayers for a meaningful life
will be granted, as will be those of many others.

An Episode of Sparrows revolves around one very real child, Lovejoy
Mason, an eleven-year-old girl whose mother, a traveling singer at her
best, pays occasional rent for her to live with the Combie family who
own a restaurant on Catford Street. Lovejoy's name suggests her illegiti-
macy—"No one who loved their child could give it a name like that,"
says Mr. Combie (26). But it also suggests her vitality. She steals, attends
school rarely, and is illiterate. Although she can remember early days
when she sang with her mother at seaside cafés in the "halcyon days
when [Lovejoy] was 'sweet'" (61), Lovejoy is somewhat embittered, living a life of neglect despite the Combies' general kindness to her. During
her mother's rare visits, Lovejoy is forced to sit outside their bedroom
while Mrs. Mason entertains "Uncle Francis" and other gentlemen.
Young as she is, she has an existential consciousness: "she had never
heard of a vortex but she knew there was a big hole, a pit, into which a
child could be swept down, a darkness that sucked her down so that she
ceased to be Lovejoy . . . and was a speck in thousands of specks," that
there was "something called 'no one'" (33).

Despite this emptiness, first experienced when her mother lost her in
London during a homeless period and nurtured during months when all
she has of her mother are postcards from faraway places, Lovejoy has a
strong core of self-integrity, very much like the seeds she bites into after
grabbing them from a smaller child's hand. "She looked at the dark part
of the seed again; it was like knowing a person was there under a dis-
guise"; she wondered, "How could it grow into a flower?" (35). This
question, signifying Lovejoy's doubts about her own survival and
growth, will be the core of the book's story—its successful outcome pre-

saged by her gesture of tucking the packet into her pocket and, despite her cynicism, the way she "began to skip home" (35).

In the course of the story, Lovejoy will increasingly become obsessed with finding good earth in which to plant the cornflower and other seeds, all the time cultivating the good earth that is, and will more fully become, herself. Yearning for a garden on hemmed-in Catford Street, she will learn that "under everything's dirt" (54), and that "dirt, earth, has power, an astonishing power of life, of creating and sweetening," of renewal, and that it can produce not only flowers but the food that is a recurrent image of life in the book. As the restaurateur Vincent Combie tells her in response to her query, "What does corn look like?": "It's a grain," and "Bread is the staff of life. . . . It can be spiritual as well as material. It's a symbol" (53).

Lovejoy's first garden is a plot of scanty earth she finds in a bombed-out ruin from which girls are excluded by a gang of boys. Nevertheless, Lovejoy clears the patch, borrowing gardening tools and even stealing money from the candle box in the Catholic church to buy more seeds. Lovejoy justifies stealing as others' irresponsibility in leaving objects or money around, but feels guilty as she imagines the statue of Mary watching her. Nevertheless, the garden flourishes, and so does Lovejoy, chanting the names of flowers like a mantra: "Love-in-a-mist, mignonette, alyssum" whenever "anything unpleasant came into her mind" (81).

One day something happens that Lovejoy cannot erase from her mind; a gang of boys burst in and in a moment destroy the garden, crushing Lovejoy's spirits as well as the flowers and grass. One boy, the strongest, is moved by Lovejoy—"he had seen the garden whole" before it was smashed and "had a vision of something laid out, green and alive" (97), of life, versus the small death created in its place. He returns to comfort Lovejoy and, in so doing, to implant the seeds of a mutually transforming relationship.

Godden is a master at creating moments of intimacy, as in this scene when the big boy Tip comforts the small girl: "The stone Tip and Lovejoy were sitting on was warm, it was the right height from the gutter to be comfortable. Scraps of conversation fell into their talk as people passed, but that only made it seem more private" (102). The sixteen-year-old boy is taken with Lovejoy. He encourages her to make another garden, and hope is restored. The garden Lovejoy wants next, she tells Tip, is "an Italian garden" (105), what Vincent Combie has pointed out in their walks, one with stone edgings and urns, a garden that is art as well as nature.

As it is for Sophie in *Kingfishers Catch Fire,* for Lovejoy and Vincent, the aesthetic impulse is primary. Vincent buys expensive dinnerware, serves a limited but superbly crafted menu (when occasional clients come to his failing restaurant, he offers them a full menu, but insists they take the "specials"—all that is available), and names himself the Italianate Vincent in place of the more mundane George. Lovejoy's garden, too, will be a work of art. Although Tip lacks artistic interests, he is ready to help pragmatically and finds a secluded spot for Lovejoy's secret garden in a cemetery behind the church. Lovejoy for once feels safe in a "sanctuary"; like Christopher Columbus, she feels an edge of hope as she discovers a new world.

The new location near the church from which she has stolen will provide an opportunity for the growth of Lovejoy's conscience. The statue of Mary overlooks the garden, and Lovejoy feels impelled to tell Tip about her theft of the candle money. Tip, a Roman Catholic boy, is shocked and agrees to give her a "penance" when Lovejoy resists his advice that she confess to Father Lambert. She must, he says, replace all the money, but not through theft; she must be barred from gardening until the debt is repaid and must enter the church eleven times to purchase candles and pray. Though Lovejoy dislikes the penance, she accepts it, and, schooled by a caring friend, she is able to develop what her mother has failed to instill in her, a sense of self-discipline.

As Lovejoy becomes more thoughtful about ethical questions—for example, is it stealing to take earth from public places? (she and Tip decide it is not)—she becomes more open to other influences. Each time she lights a candle, she finds herself praying. At first she asks for money to complete her penance, and even this mundane prayer is answered, seemingly as a result of the intensity of her need. A handsome, wealthy couple are visiting the church—"Somebodies," "Real People" (120) in Lovejoy's eyes—and as Lovejoy turns around, they hand her a shilling. Prayer begets answered prayer, and answered prayer more prayer as Lovejoy invests the shilling in another candle to pay off her debt, inspiring the lady benefactor to see her as a "a little saint." While Lovejoy is no saint, neither is she, as the lady's man friend jests, "a little sinner, more likely" (124). Rather, she is a girl in transition, trying to become a "somebody," a "real person," trying to find her own ballast.

This couple, Charles and Liz, will later make one of Lovejoy's most extravagant wishes come true. Now that penance is complete, Lovejoy, with Tip's help, keeps working up the new garden site. Insisting that she needs "good garden earth" and that it can be gotten only from the square,

Lovejoy, along with Tip and Sparkey, makes midnight excursions to climb into the public garden and fill thirteen buckets with earth. As Vincent tells Lovejoy, "Wanting is the beginning of getting," and the reason people don't get things is that "they don't work hard enough" (145). Surely, the children do work hard—"it was very far from play" (144)—and in so doing, bring about their own fulfillment. As the Chinese proverb Godden quotes observes, "Who plants a garden plants happiness" (14).

Almost twenty years later, Rumer Godden was to publish a children's book called *The Old Woman Who Lived in a Vinegar Bottle* (1972), the story of which she relates in brief in *An Episode of Sparrows*. In sum, it is the tale of an old woman who lived in a vinegar bottle (she was embittered) and found six pence, which she used to buy a fish. Since it was a small fish, she threw it back into the river and it granted her unlimited favors in gratitude. The old woman kept returning to the river to ask for first small and then larger and larger favors, all of which were granted until the fish became tired. So with Lovejoy: having had the basic wish for a garden granted, she now feels a higher Maslowian need for the aesthetic. "We must have something special" (145), she tells Tip. Tip gives her his pocket money, the kindergarten teacher gives her six packets of grass seeds, and a neighbor, Mr. Manley, underwrites her loan at the seed shop, but it is Charles and Liz who give her something special in the form of a miniature rosebush.

One day, Charles and Liz invite Lovejoy for a ride in their car. In Liz's arms is a miniature rosebush, like the one Lovejoy has seen in a neighbor's catalogue. Sensing the intensity of Lovejoy's yearning for something she never knew really existed, Charles and Liz exchange glances and "set it in Lovejoy's lap" (163). This is one of those moments in Godden's writing that give her work an extraordinary poignancy, which derives from the power of extreme longing unexpectedly fulfilled. "When the heavens open one does not say thank you." Lovejoy can only gaze "dumbly at the rose" until Charles brings her back to reality as he says, "You're in the car . . . you must get out now" (163); Charles and Liz provide, for a moment, a model of ideal surrogate parents, reading a child's mind and filling her deepest desire, as Sophie would say, "without stint." And it is not only Lovejoy's longing that is fulfilled by this couple, but Vincent's as well, for they visit his restaurant, and in their regal appreciation of his culinary talents provide him with a model of the ideal clientele that he believes he deserves, motivating him, despite his wife's warning, to purchase an expensive refrigerator to prepare for more clients of their caliber.

But as in *The Old Woman Who Lived in a Vinegar Bottle,* the universal fish cannot be relied on to fulfill wants interminably. Some self-regulatory process is necessary in the "wanter." When Vincent sees Charles's and Liz's car parked outside the church (they are planning to contribute money toward its rebuilding), he mistakenly assumes they will visit his restaurant and impulsively purchases ingredients for a lavish meal. When he realizes the meal will be wasted, his disappointment and the financial loss incurred spur the decline of his restaurant, which, with a second blow—the disappearance of Lovejoy's mother and the small income she contributed—leads to the closing of the restaurant and the Combies' decision to put Lovejoy in a children's home.

A third blow comes simultaneously when Tip is captured taking earth from the square and Lovejoy runs away to bring the earth to the garden to nourish her cherished rosebush. While Tip will ultimately forgive Lovejoy, he believes she has abandoned him out of selfishness, not understanding that for her saving the garden is the highest good, that for Lovejoy the garden represents a transcendent entity, a triumph over selfishness.

Later, when Lovejoy appears at the police precinct to look for Tip, she meets Angela and Olivia for the first time. While Angela lodges a complaint about the children's theft of earth, which she has observed from her window, Olivia forms a silent bond with Lovejoy. When a policewoman approaches Lovejoy to tell her that her mother has gone away for good, Lovejoy's newly achieved self-integrity is threatened, and she sees the vortex before her, "thousands and thousands of little ant people being swept into it" (195). Instinctively, she reaches out for Olivia's hand, and Olivia, who has also known what it feels like to be a "pinprick" in a teeming universe, feels made real.

While Angela helps make arrangements for Lovejoy to enter the children's home and continues to insist on prosecuting Tip for theft and assault, the protective forces in the universe are also at work. Father Lambert has been watching Lovejoy's garden grow and now supports Olivia's claim that the garden is "innocent," a "little garden almost in a church" (205–6) made in the rubble that nobody wanted, where nobody "saw." This "seeing"—which Godden often refers to elsewhere as *darshan* and which for her is a holy, a visionary recognition of the essence of what is seen—now becomes of utmost importance to Lovejoy's future.

The garden (and by extension the children) is indeed innocent, says Father Lambert. You need only look at it in the right way to see: "If you bend down, about the height of a child, and look, then you can see what it is." While Angela's pride will not permit her to stoop to this view,

Olivia can see it all: "There are paths of marble chips . . . and edgings of stone, and a lawn of mustard and cress; they had a wreath-case for a flowerpot and a little column with ivy growing up it, truly beautiful" (206).

When Angela scorns her for this speech, and their friend Mr. Wix tries to comfort her by saying, "You are taking this far too much to heart," she retorts, "Isn't that where we should take it?" (207). Olivia now feels the pain near her heart that signals both her terminal illness and the depth of her feeling, a pain that will bring her a profound revelation. When Wix offers glib comfort, "We must trust . . . not one sparrow can fall to the ground," Olivia cries out, "But they fall all the time. . . . We knock them, crush them . . . and they fall. That's what humans do to humans, so don't talk to me about God." The revelation that the reader feels with the same force as Olivia is a basic truth that loses all abstractness in the context of the book: "Humans to humans?" And, as if she had just found out something, she asks, "Is that how it works? Someone, one person at least, is meant to see the fall and care?" One person must "see and become the instrument. I have seen . . . I shall keep my eyes open in spite of you" (208).

This vow gives her the determination to live a while longer despite her diagnosis, long enough to ensure that Lovejoy's story has a happy ending. Things seem bleakest when Lovejoy is taken to the ironically named House of Compassion. As Angela explains, it is a "home for children who are to be pitied" (234), children who have nothing but what other kind people give them. Lovejoy responds, "Yes, I have to have kind people" (235), implying a very different definition of kindness and perhaps Godden's Blakean rejection of that "pity" that perpetuates the need for charity.

Wishing to be the opposite of what the children's home would have her be, "Quiet, obedient, grateful," Lovejoy prays, "Hail Mary," "make me cocky and independent" (238). The restaurant is boarded up, the church is torn down, and corpses are unearthed in the rubble. When Olivia's will is read, however, all is redeemed. The restaurant is to be reopened, managed by Vincent, on the condition that a legacy left in the Combies' care be used to support Lovejoy. Tip, who has been sent to naval training school by his benefactor, the admiral, may visit Lovejoy at will. The admiral shows off the children's garden to members of the Committee for the Improvement of Society, noting that "the holes are closing up; we didn't do anything, they're closing themselves, making new earth. Don't ask me how . . . because I don't know" (247). Indeed, *An Episode of Sparrows* attests to the fact that if there is only someone to bear witness, to see, as Olivia sees Lovejoy, as the admiral sees Tip, as Father Lambert continues to see and bless both children, overall healing can and will take place for those who have been abandoned, enabling both young and old to close up the inner holes in the fabric of the self.

The Greengage Summer

Unlike Lovejoy, the four children in *The Greengage Summer* (1958) are only temporarily abandoned by their mother, but this hiatus in parenting produces a gap in which tremendous changes take place in the children's internal growth. Based on Rumer Godden's childhood experience, noted in *A Time to Dance, No Time to Weep,* when Katherine Godden took her children on a trip to the battlefields of Normandy to inspire them to be less selfish, *The Greengage Summer* tells the story of children effectively abandoned by their mother when she, like Mrs. Godden, becomes ill in France. They are left on their own to cope with an unknown environment that offers excitement, danger, and the potential for growth.

Joss, sixteen; Cecil (the narrator), thirteen; and Vicky, Hester, and Willmouse Grey, the younger siblings, are, like the Godden children, stultified by life in England (in the novel, Southstone) and by their Uncle William. Kind but conventional, William cannot comprehend why artistic Joss, sensitive Cecil, and unboyish Willmouse (he loves to dress up in girl's clothing and dress dolls—he has the soul of a designer) are miserable in a world that is all "middle, middle, middle"[7] and crave the larger, less predictable world.

The Grey father is, for all purposes, absent, off in Tibet studying botany on three-year tours. Their mother is described as "like a child, transparently aboveboard and open" (15), but the narrator suspects that she might be wise as well. She does remove Willmouse from the boys' school he hates and recognizes that as an effectively single parent, she must do something to save her children from the rudeness their dissatisfaction with life in Southstone has fostered in them. Her notion of showing them the fields of martyrdom is meant to demonstrate that some people have sacrificed their lives for the well-being of others. But the trip will also serve to remove the children from the narrow environment in which they—and she—have been encapsulated. As Cecil will comment on waking in the French hotel for the first time, "To wake for the first time in a new place can be like another birth" (31).

In France the children will receive an education, but it will not be as simple as the one Mrs. Grey had in mind. Their educational journey begins when the family arrives in France and Mrs. Grey immediately falls ill from an insect bite. The children, stranded in the train station, are forced to hospitalize their mother and find lodgings for themselves. They make their way to Les Oeillets (L'Hotel des Violettes of Godden's childhood) on the Marne, a onetime chateau, now a hotel. The surroundings at Les Oeillets are different from the deadly battlefields of their original destination, for the hotel is encircled by fecund gardens overflowing with the smell of ripe greengage plum trees. The children's gorging on the fruit of these trees, while confirming their mother's diagnosis of greed, will become a symbol of the exotic sensuousness of the world into which they will be introduced, of the experience that will penetrate their eyes (*oeilles*) as well as their other senses. They will taste the fruit of the tree of knowledge of good and evil provided by the seemingly Edenic setting.

The good and evil the children will taste is largely embodied in the character of Eliot, the mysterious, romantic figure who is the hotel manager's friend. It is he, who, from the moment he recognizes them as abandoned—"Good God," he remarks on first sight, "an orphanage" (7)—takes the children under his wing, protecting them from the jealous manager, Mademoiselle Zizi, making sure they and their mother are cared for, and recognizing their individual needs (he provides Willmouse with art books, including a big book of old masters that he advises the boy to study for design qualities). Near the end of the book, in loco parenti, he will send for their Uncle William; then Eliot will flee to escape the police, who come to arrest him as the infamous robber and murderer he is under his charming exterior.

Grown-ups, Joss is to observe, "are like icebergs, three-tenths showing, seven-tenths submerged" (15), causing pain to children who unknowingly collide with them. As the children spend time at Les Oeillets, their eyes are forcibly opened to the reality underlying the surface of things. As the translated name of the hotel suggests—"The House of Eyes"—seeing is at the heart of the book. The children will learn that "nothing was what it seemed," that the hotel itself, advertised as the site of many battles, is built on falsehood. The skulls unearthed in the garden have been planted and replanted there, and the bloodstained walls and bullet holes have been freshened up regularly. Mademoiselle Zizi and Eliot are lovers, and Mademoiselle Zizi, though she has a childlike name, is not childlike; her feet are calloused and ugly compared with Joss's, and so is her soul. Eliot himself can be unexpectedly cold and rejecting at times, but recklessly flirts with Joss at others. And, at the end, he is revealed as a criminal.

There is a hedge separating the false tourists' garden from the unspoiled truth in the field beyond. It is Eliot who observes that "as soon as a human goes out into the morning it is spoilt" (34), except for artists and children. It is in this field, beyond the house, in which Eliot picnics and feasts on greengages with the children and into which M. Joubert the artist disappears "in the wilderness" to paint.

When Joss recovers (she had also been sick earlier on, leaving the narrator, Cecil, at the center of the book to create her own vision of herself and of Les Oeillets), M. Joubert recognizes her artistic abilities (which parallel those of Godden's sister Jon), and insists that she quietly paint with him every day. Joss finds a place for herself, reveling in the respect shown her as she is treated as an adult. Cecil and the other children have also found their private directions each day and, in pursuit of them, each day become more themselves. Children, the implication is, are best off if placed in an environment that offers them challenging resources for the development of self and are then largely ignored. But unlike Rousseau's Emile, whose ideal environment was closely monitored as he grew and suffered the sometimes carefully orchestrated "natural consequences" of his actions, Godden's child characters must draw on their own inner resources to cope with the negatives as well as the positives in their strange environment.

Eliot takes the children on long excursions, to vineyards, to the Forest of Compiègne, and to a village with a castle-like chateau "like the Sleeping Beauty's," leading the narrator to comment on the "fairy-tale day" they've shared. When Joss denies it is a fairy tale, asserting, "It's true," Eliot, taking her arm, agrees, "It is true"; the reader, however, catches a glimpse of strong undercurrents, of an attraction between Eliot and Joss, of little flirtations between them unnoticed or denied by the narrator, who comments, "I could see it was not possible for Joss to walk arm in arm with him, and as soon as she could, she took her arm away" (103).

Mademoiselle Zizi, however, has no difficulty in recognizing Eliot's interest in Joss. She tries to relegate the sixteen-year-old girl to the status of a child to keep the borderline between child and adult barricaded: "Who gave you permission to change your time for dinner . . . who said you could change?" (89) she asks, ordering the children to eat with the servants, who, like children, are members of an underclass. Joss resists being blocked from change, from growth. She "could have taken refuge in being small, a child," but instead responds, "I am as big as I am" (90), pointing out that Eliot and her mother would not approve of the children's dining with the servants. Although Joss wins the battle, the war continues, and when Eliot and the children return from Compiègne, Eliot has to ply Mademoiselle Zizi with drinks to dampen her jealousy, leading the narrator to comment, from the perspective of the adult writer, "I know now it is children who accept life, grown people cover it up and pretend it is different with drinks" (107).

Her inability to accept Joss's "change" into an adult leads Zizi to falsely accuse Joss of sexual intimacy with M. Joubert and to force the painter to leave the hotel. Mademoiselle Zizi's jealousy proves Eliot's point about adults ruining the morning. It provokes Joss to adopt a seductive manner to persuade a male guest to escort her to a dinner party from which Mademoiselle Zizi has banned her. As a result, Cecil begins to feel that "things are no longer truthful" (163). With burgeoning adulthood comes conscious deceptiveness. The borderline between good and evil, innocence and experience, childhood and adulthood is an invisible one, easily and sometimes unknowingly crossed, but once crossed, almost impossible to retrace.

Although the children increasingly become aware of Eliot's lies, when Joss wants to return to England, Cecil begs her not to. "We are alive" here, she argues. "Don't you feel as if you were being stretched?" Joss replies, "It hurts to be stretched" (125). Cecil is literally hurting, experiencing the growing pains that will signal her first menstruation. Despite everything, she will confide in Eliot, who will give her exactly what she needs to feel able to enter womanhood: "It hurts," she tells him. "Not when you consider how exciting it is," he responds, "because now you are ready for love." He makes her feel pretty (167). It is Eliot's ability to help the children be themselves that leads Cecil to feel that she is being stretched and to wonder whether it is possible to love a bad person.

The denouement comes quickly. With her new sense of womanhood come new fears as well. One night, Cecil senses someone about to enter her window. It is Paul, the young servant, who in a moment disappears with a cry. Eliot, who has been preparing to flee, has apprehended Paul, and when they fight, Paul is killed and Eliot runs off. In her new state of awareness, Cecil is witness to a scene that is complex and, to her, incomprehensible.

It turns out that Eliot, who is really the master burglar Allen, has taken a barge down the Marne to escape the Inspector, who, having recognized him at Compiègne, is in pursuit. But when Uncle William suddenly appears at the hotel, the children learn that Eliot has taken time to send him a telegram, urging him to come. This telegram gives the Inspector a clue as to Eliot's path of escape, leaving open the question of whether Eliot will be apprehended as a result of his altruism. The children return to Southstone changed, pondering Cecil's question about the complexities of human nature. They have discovered new aspects of themselves. Joss sends the Inspector the photo of Eliot her sister Hester had taken, so the children are in some sense accomplices in the possible doom of the man they have cared for. This complicity makes them realize that they have eaten of the tree of knowledge of good and evil and have been transformed from a state of innocence to experience. As Joss observes, with an emphasis on the children's internal changes implied in the pronoun, "*We* never came back" to Southstone (6).

Children figure centrally in Godden's novels of the 1950s. Except for the Mousewife and Sophie, adults are, on the whole, peripheral figures, and all, including the Mousewife and Sophie, are frustrated in their ambitions. In these books, although adults may reach out to fulfill wants, circumstances generally force them back home. How do children react to this pessimistic reality? Unlike Bogey in *The River*, who has no "wants" and dies young, Teresa, Lovejoy, and Cecil continue to want and to "will"—to strive to realize their desires through sheer force of will—deeply; there is an underlying sense in the books of this decade that the complex view of human nature and the self achieved by child protagonists through experience may enable them to meet the challenges of adulthood with better success than their elders.

Chapter Four
Doll Stories, 1954–1964

Children and young adults in Godden's nonjuvenile books are often exposed to experiences that are, like greengage plums, too rich to be digested easily. In *An Episode of Sparrows,* the garden serves as a mitigating symbol of Lovejoy's growth and transformation; in *The Greengage Summer,* there is only the motif of the children's journey to Les Oeillets ("The House of Eyes," or "I's") and the ambivalent figure of Eliot (a near-anagram for Oeillet) to help Cecil navigate the dangerous waters of enlarged perception.

A group of dolls' books written and published over a period of about ten years provides a bridge between the 1950s and 1960s. Frank Eyre says of Godden's first doll story, *The Dolls' House,* that it "brilliantly succeeds in depicting adult situations and conflicts in a story that on the surface is no more than a simple tale"[1] and that it "communicates a surprising amount about human nature and the drama and tragedy of adult life" (80). His remarks might well be extended to all of Godden's doll stories.

As Lois Kuznets points out, in Godden's doll stories, "somehow solutions to the children's needs and conflicts come in tandem with the resolution of doll problems."[2] Indeed, as suggested earlier, Godden's work provides a series of mirrors in which children's inner conflicts and changing self-images are reflected in miniature in the figures of the dolls and mice of the children's books and in sometimes overwhelming enlargement in the full-scale figures of adult fiction. Thus, in discussing the seven doll stories of the 1950s and 1960s, various relationships must be considered: the dolls to one another; the children and the dolls; the children, dolls, and any adults in the story; and the child and adult reader's relationship to all of these.

Impunity Jane

Each of the stories collected in the book *Four Dolls* (1983)—*Impunity Jane* (1954), *The Fairy Doll* (1956), *The Story of Holly and Ivy* (1958), and *Candy Floss* (1960)—develops the theme Godden observes in *Holly and*

Ivy, that "wishes are powerful things."³ Impunity Jane is a four-inch china doll who sits in a toy store with telescopes, sailing ships, and active toys. This doll reflects a conflict about the feminine role. On the one hand, Impunity longs for adventure and feels she will "crack" if she doesn't get some. Her strength is suggested by Effie's grandmother (grandmothers tend to be strong women in Godden's work), who buys the doll as a gift for her grandchild. Impunity, grandmother tells Effie, is strong and can be dropped "with impunity" or "without hurt." On the other hand, Effie defines *imp* as a "naughty little magic person" (7), thereby qualifying the nature of the doll's strength.

Impunity Jane is largely ignored, as Effie prefers "pressing flowers" to playing active games with her. Succeeding generations of little girls inherit the doll: Elizabeth, who dresses her up in clothes that cut like a knife; Ethel, who teaches her reading, writing, and arithmetic; and Ellen, who is a modern child, "too busy to play" (13), and keeps the dolls' house shut. It is only when a boy cousin, Gideon, arrives that Impunity is treated as she wishes.

Gideon places the dolls' house in a tree for the birds to nest in and floats it downriver on a raft; he even carries Impunity in his pocket. Gideon seems to feel Impunity's wishes, and the doll experiences the world through his eyes. Like some other small boys (Willmouse in *The Greengage Summer* and Bogey in *The River*), Gideon is not an altogether traditional boy, but he cleverly justifies playing with a doll by presenting it to his peers as a model figure to ride in boats and so forth.

Soon, however, Impunity feels guilty about Gideon's having removed her from the dolls' house and masochistically forces herself to wish him to put her back in it. He does, and she cracks. Fortunately, the broken doll is given to Gideon when he asks for it, and he mends and keeps her. Ellen, the girl who gives Impunity to Gideon, is not interested in dolls. In this reversal of traditional roles, Ellen's lack of interest in dolls may suggest that as a modern young lady, she has already achieved the independence Impunity craves. For Gideon, on the other hand, Impunity represents the affective aspect of the self that boys have traditionally been encouraged to suppress.

The Fairy Doll

If in *Impunity Jane* a boy gives vicarious life to a female doll, in *The Fairy Doll* a female doll becomes a young girl's inner guide, speaking to her, and giving her confidence and the ability to wish and to achieve. Slow, fat Elizabeth, who is four years old, feels different from her three older siblings and is mocked by them and by her schoolmates. Only she senses that the fairy doll on top of the Christmas tree is alive and that her wand stirs minutely. She eagerly awaits Christmas each year for the fairy doll's visit. When Elizabeth's great-grandmother comes to visit, she is described as being very much like the fairy doll, and it is unclear whether the voice Elizabeth hears is her grandmother's or the doll's.

Whatever the source of the voice, the fairy doll falls at great-grandmother's feet and great-grandmother gives her to Elizabeth, saying, "you needed a good fairy" (46). Elizabeth makes a house for the fairy doll in her bike basket and takes her everywhere, asking her questions, the response to which is a "ting" that goes off in her head and a "funny feeling like a hard little wand" that stirs in her, telling her just what to do and how to do it. Thus, she learns to brush her teeth, do math, read, and be clever. One day, Elizabeth loses the fairy doll and is disconsolate. But when great-grandmother comes, Elizabeth hears the "ting" again and learns that the sound is truly within her own self. Once having achieved that insight, Elizabeth even finds the fairy doll again, but now she is confident enough of her own resources to put the doll back in the Christmas box until the following year.

As the Rustins observe in *Narratives of Love and Loss,* "the fairy doll is able to be the 'container' for many of the child's ideas and feelings" (92). Once Elizabeth is able to integrate her negative and positive feelings into a more confident self, she no longer needs the external projection to develop independently.

The Story of Holly and Ivy

The Story of Holly and Ivy opens with the words, "This is a story about wishing" (68). Here, the wishes of girl and doll are equally strong, and the two entities are equally helpful to one another. Six-year-old Ivy is an orphan who longs to spend Christmas with an imagined grandmother. Holly is a Christmas doll who lives in a shop with other toys awaiting Christmas purchase. Sometimes "in Ivy there was an empty feeling, and the emptiness ached" (73). It is this loneliness that leads her to detrain to seek her imaginary grandmother before reaching the charitable institution to which she is being sent for the holidays. Ivy's intense internal wishing leads her to Holly and also seems to draw a third being to the shopwindow: the childless Mrs. Jones, who sees Ivy and longs to spend Christmas with a little girl.

Meanwhile, Ivy sees Holly and Holly sees Ivy, and both wish intently for a miracle to bring them together. Ivy helps Peter, who works in the toy store, find the key he has lost in the snow, and thereby meets Mrs. Jones's husband, a policeman, who is at the scene. When Ivy tells Mr. Jones that she is looking for her grandmother's house and leads him to his own home (earlier, she had spotted the grandmotherly Mrs. Jones preparing Christmas dinner), Ivy's wish (and Mrs. Jones's) is granted. Ivy and Holly are equally delighted when Peter gives Holly to Ivy as a present. Peter had tried to bring other dolls as a gift, but each doll had pricked him or in some way made it inevitable that Holly be chosen. Holly and Ivy are fated to belong to each other, as are Ivy and Mr. and Mrs. Jones. As already noted, for Godden wishes are powerful things; particularly for her child characters, positive visualization pays off in the end.

Candy Floss

If "wishes are powerful things" in *Candy Floss,* they can also be dangerous things. Clementina Davenport, a rich girl for whom "I want" means "I shall" learns that "having everything you want can make you very tired" (121). Seven-year-old Clementina wants to buy Candy Floss, a pretty blue-eyed doll belonging to Jack, the man who runs a booth at the fair. After Clementina snatches Candy Floss and runs away with her, Candy Floss resists her kidnapper by setting her will against Clementina when the girl tries to change her clothes or feed her. As Candy Floss has determined, Clementina comes to feel the doll's will, for Clementina is not used to resistance. At one point her resistance to Clementina's assault on her leads Candy Floss to sicken; she cracks, her eyes loosen, and she loses her shine. Clementina discards her on the road, but the music of the fair reaches her, seeming to judge her—"Cruel Clementina" (131). Now Clementina sickens, feeling guilty despite herself. Candy Floss, a doll, to all appearances devoid of feeling, has made a real girl feel. Clementina returns Candy Floss to Jack and asks him for a job, signaling her increasing sense of responsibility and maturity.

Miss Happiness and Miss Flower

Miss Happiness and Miss Flower (1961) is the story of two Japanese dolls, each about five inches high, their faces and hands made of "white plaster, their bodies of rag,"[4] sent as a gift to two cousins, Belinda and Nona Fell, in England. The dolls, whose previous life is unclear, experience anxiety about their new home and wish for a "kind girl" to take care of them. Like Rumer and her sisters, they seem to have lived in many places and are somewhat disoriented—"'Where are we now?' asked Miss Flower. 'Is it another country?'" Nona shares in the dolls' sense of confusion, loneliness, and powerlessness. A dark-skinned orphan (like Ripsie in *China Court,* published in the same year), Nona has been sent out of India to live with her aunt and uncle, without having any say in the matter. As Miss Happiness responds when Miss Flower murmurs, "I wish we had not come"—"We were not asked" (2). Nona's name is indicative of her lonely, negative nature, for she says, "No" to everything—food, school, and play. But when she sees the dolls, she subconsciously begins to respond to their wishes for kindness and starts to stroke Miss Flowers's chipped face in sympathy.

Belinda Fell, like Clementina in *Candy Floss,* lacks Nona's sympathetic nature and will need to be tempered in the course of the story. Deriding the dolls because "They're not even new" (6), she is also mean and condescending to Nona, making fun of her when she describes how Japanese children celebrate the Star Festival by writing wishes on paper and tying them to bamboos outside the house. Nona ties her own wishes to trees, to the immense but secret enjoyment of the dolls, who quietly begin to wish for their own house.

Perhaps responding subconsciously but imperfectly to the dolls' wishes, Belinda puts the dolls in her dolls' house, where they feel uncomfortable in the Western setting. Nona recognizes their discomfort and wants to make them their own home. That children can help children becomes evident when Nona is empowered by Belinda's brother, Tom, who tells her, "You could make a dolls'-house" (16), and that everything necessary can be learned from books. Mr. Twilfit, the ornery bookseller, becomes an older helping figure in the tale as he allows Nona to borrow a book on dolls' houses.

Strengthened by the project, Nona responds to the dolls' unspoken wishes that she go to school to learn how to read house-building instructions and weave mats for their new home. That she is able to take Miss Happiness and Miss Flower with her in her head to comfort herself suggests that Nona has progressed to the point where absent objects have been internalized and that she is learning to overcome loss.

Nona's discomfort in the Fell household is mirrored by the dolls' unhappiness in Belinda's dolls' house, and the silent communication between Nona and the dolls strengthens both child and dolls. The more overt communication from Tom to Nona, in which he lends her his "masculine" confidence, leads her to realize she can create a house in which her internal world and external objects can live comfortably. In Godden's doll stories, children must find ways to build bridges between feelings and the objective world, both of which can be represented by the dolls, and to integrate so-called masculine and feminine sides of the personality. Because of her insecurity, Nona wishes she were a boy (as Godden sometimes did as a child), but of course it may really be the empowerment traditionally associated with masculinity that she craves—and that is what she finally achieves.

That Belinda, despite her outward show of confidence, is also insecure is suggested when, feeling left out, she claims Miss Flower as her own and puts her back in the Western-style dolls' house. Miss Happiness silently cries, "I'm afraid that Miss Flower will not be able to bear it. I'm afraid she will break." Indeed, there is an ominous silence—"There was certainly not a sound or movement in Belinda's dolls' house; not the smallest doll rustle" (66). This silence, resembling death, represents the symbolic death of Belinda's selfishness, as, chastised and ignored by her family, she is left alone in the house of her self. There, "she cried herself awake, perhaps more awake than she had ever been in her life." For the first time, she thinks of someone else: "What did I do to Miss Flower?" (68) and tenderly puts her back in the Japanese dolls' house where she belongs.

Now Belinda can wish, too, saying, "I wish there were something for me" (71). She learns that wishes can immediately be granted when her parents give her a golden peach. When opened, the peach reveals inside the tiny boy-doll figurine of Little Peach, which Belinda has long wanted. It is fitting that the dolls are named Flower and Happiness, for both girls have flowered into happiness as a result of their interactions with each other, with the dolls, and with the helping figures of Tom and Mr. Twilfit. At the conclusion of the book, readers of *Miss Happiness and Little Flower* are provided with instructions for building a Japanese dolls' house so that they, too, may find happiness and fruition through the self-empowerment of house building.

Little Plum

Little Plum (1963) takes up a year later, where *Miss Happiness and Miss Flower* end, but here Belinda is more center stage. The Fell family—which includes Nona, now nine, as well as her cousins, Belinda, eight; Tom, twelve; and Anne, fifteen—is fascinated by "The House Next

Door," which is referred to as "Derelict" and which the book defines as "Empty." Much as the Japanese house in the previous book and Mouse House and China Court in Godden's books of those names serve as symbols of the fulfilled self in relationship to others, so the emptiness of the house next door represents the constricted life of the girl who will soon move into it. Gem Tiffany Jones, whose first two names belie her barren life but foreshadow her development through the course of the book, lives with her strict aunt and saddened father, whose wife is hospitalized, paralyzed by polio.

Deprived of good mothering, Gem is herself paralyzed emotionally, and she appropriates her aunt's condescending attitude toward the children next door, especially toward tomboy Belinda. But though Belinda still has an aggressive side, it has been tempered by warm feeling. When spying on Gem from the ilex tree, which serves as a boundary between the two houses, Belinda discovers that Gem, too, has a Japanese doll but that she never plays with it, Belinda determines that "Nothing is worse for a doll than not to be played with"[5] and decides to make a coat for the doll, whom she names Little Plum. For Belinda, thought equals action; using her problem-solving abilities, she figures out how to get the clothes to Little Plum: "If I could slide, say, a plank, or something, across until one end was on the fire escape, the other on the fork, then I could stand on the landing on one foot, put my other foot on that drain-pipe; I could hold on to the fire-escape railing with one hand," and "I believe I could just, just reach the window ledge" (52). Full of an initiative that fully integrates masculine and feminine aspects of self, Belinda cuts a "length of rope from the boys' store with Anne's Girl Guide knife that she was not supposed to touch" (55), earning Miss Flower's warm, silent admiration—"Little Miss is as brave as a dragon!" (57).

In the series of succeeding messages Belinda leaves Gem—"CAN'T YOU KEEP YOUR DOLL WORME [*sic*]" (57) and "Why don't you give your poor starving doll some FOOD" (62)—and in the answers Gem returns— "MIND YOUR OWN BUSINESS" (57) and "Trespassers will be prosecuted" (60)—it is clear that more fundamental issues are being debated than the doll's care; Gem's entire care and well-being are on the line (literally, as Belinda hangs between her house and the "derelict one," striving for some form of communication).

Will Gem allow the true jewel of self to be burnished, permitting her starved nature to partake of the warmth and nourishment of friendship, or will her overdeveloped negative superego force her to react angrily and remain an "empty house"? It certainly seems that the latter will be

the case as Gem rejects nourishment for Little Plum and sends back a
mixture of bad food (a written recipe, with ingredients such as roaches,
vinegar, and worms); still, the exchange of words, however nasty, is a
form of communication.

Miss Happiness and Miss Flower worry about Little Plum being
caught in the middle of this warfare, much as Godden's own children in
Kashmir and Teresa in *Kingfishers Catch Fire* feel overwhelmed by quarrelling. But in dolls' books, dolls can serve as powerful mediators of
quarrels, and Belinda's kidnapping of Little Plum to hide her in the
Japanese dolls' house so that she can care for her properly will lead to
conciliation.

When through her window Belinda sees Gem crying disconsolately
for Little Plum, she climbs the tree again to return the doll but becomes
paralyzed when she's observed by the Jones family. Only when Mr.
Tiffany Jones urges her on—"Brave girl"—is she able to move. "You
won't fall. . . . Look straight at me," Mr. Tiffany Jones commands.
When Belinda fearfully answers, "I'm going to fall," Gem's father
responds, "Fall? With Gem looking?" (78). Here Belinda has almost suc-
cumbed to a paralysis similar to that of Gem's mother, who is stricken
not only with polio but with a profound feeling of hopelessness produced
by the emptiness of her life with her husband and his sister, who has
come to live with them. Now, as Mr. Tiffany Jones regards Belinda, she
is reempowered, for his saving attention validates and reinforces her
efforts to save his daughter. His statement that Belinda cannot fall with
Gem looking is not only an appeal to Belinda's narcissism but a suggestion that she has finally caught Gem's attention and that Gem's recov-
ery from emotional paralysis hangs with Belinda on the limb.

The book concludes with a Japanese Festival of Dolls the Fell girls
hold with the assistance of Mr. Twilfit. Belinda invites Little Plum, with
a note to "please bring your most Honourable Girl" (88). Gem's mother
makes a surprise appearance at the feast in a wheelchair, and when her
sister-in-law asks why she wasn't informed of the feast and of Mrs.
Tiffany Jones's arrival, Gem's mother replies, referring to Little Plum
and Gem as well as to herself, "You see, you don't have to tell people
when you come home" (96). The nanny is dismissed as Gem discovers
she herself can nurture others: "I don't need someone to look after me,"
for "I have to look after Mother" (97). Here, Gem's mother's expression
of strength and support, mysteriously facilitated by Gem's development
(why does the mother appear at this felicitous moment?), enables Gem
to nurture her mother and, concurrently, herself. Through the mediation

of the dolls, the house next door is no longer "derelict." Signals are now sent from house to house each night, saying "Sayonara," with sounds that resemble the girls' voices. As the author tells us, however, they are really those of the dolls—that is, the true inner and interactive life of the self. It is in this house with four rooms that the child and adult reader must ultimately feel comfortable.

As already noted, Rumer Godden observes in her most recent autobiography that we all live in four rooms, the mental, physical, emotional, and spiritual. Belinda has demonstrated her capacity to move freely through these four rooms, through mental exertion (problem solving), physical exertion (tree climbing), emotional extension (sympathy for Little Plum and both anger and sympathy for Gem), and spiritual connection (silent communication with the dolls). Just as Gem begins to fill her house more fully after "looking" at Belinda, so, too, may child and adult readers be mysteriously moved to fill all the corners of their own houses of the self after reading *Little Plum* and Rumer Godden's other doll books.

Home Is the Sailor

Yet another doll book of the 1960s is *Home Is the Sailor* (1964). In this book, children recede into the background, and the focus is on the activities and feelings of the dolls who live in a dolls' house in Wales. The dolls include Curly, a seven-year-old sailor doll "with a mop of curled gold hair, and blue glass eyes";[6] Morello, a servant with a "miserable nature" (like Marchpane in *The Dolls' House*); the baby, Bundle; the saddened governess, Charlotte (the mother of the dolls' mistress gave Miss Charlotte's sailor fiancé Thomas away to a little French girl years ago); the celluloid servant, Mrs. Lewis; and fearful Mrs. Raleigh, the head of the house, who refuses to go on picnics because her husband, Captain Raleigh, was lost on one.

The dolls and the real child, Sian, seem unhappy—the dolls because there is no man doll in the house (Morello nastily predicts there never will be) and Sian because there is some failure in human communication in her busy home: "Sian would have been very lonely, if it had not been for the dolls' house; in fact, the dolls seemed more alive and companionable than real people to Sian" (22). To lift everyone's spirits, Curly determines to go to sea to find and bring back Thomas. Mrs. Lewis wishes for a child to place Curly near the telescope on the human family's roof, and when that wish is fulfilled, Curly is able to fall or be blown out the window (sometimes even dolls' wishes can mysteriously translate into action). He is picked up by Bertrand, an obnoxious French boy, a super-perfectionist, who has been sent to sea school in Wales to get him out of his family's hair.

Bertrand, who has suffered a loss of self-esteem after the boys at school ragged him for his pretentiousness, feels suddenly stronger and more self-aware when he picks up Curly. He realizes that he had been sent to England by his parents and then to Wales by his aunt and uncle because they wanted to get rid of him; he wonders why nobody seems to like him. His internal reflections make him aware that he "had been making—a lot of noise . . . teaching people, airing his opinions, telling people all the time what they ought to do." He looks at Curly, who, "whatever colour he was [he changes color in different lights], he looked the same Curly, happy and cheerful, and he made Bertrand feel ashamed" (66).

As Bertrand carries Curly in his pocket, his heart aching with self-doubt and a feeling of unlovableness, "it was comforting to have the weight of Curly" (66). In *Impunity Jane,* the doll is a "model" in two ways for Gideon and helps him integrate the male and female sides of his nature. Curly is "more than a mascot" for the much more needy Bertrand; he is a toy, a "buddy," but, most important, Curly is an objectification of the cheerfully balanced nature that Bertrand now hopes to achieve. When Curly falls again, this time out of Bertrand's pocket into the sea, Bertrand jumps in to save him.

In saving Curly, Bertrand is, in one sense, saving his own highest self. He will emerge from his baptism a better boy. But the doll Curly needs Bertrand as much as Bertrand needs him, and Curly wishes "as he had never wished before" not to sink, that Bertrand would come. When Bertrand does reach for Curly, his hand appears as "something large and pale, not unlike the starfish but a hundred times bigger" (72). Bertrand is reflected in Curly's eyes as an ideal being, and indeed Bertrand's false perfectionism has been replaced with a more real heroism.

Bertrand's and Curly's reciprocal acts of salvation and heroism seem to serve as a catalyst for others' acts of restitution in the story. While walking on the beach, Sian stumbles on Captain Raleigh and brings him home. As Sian remarks, "It will be a great shock" to Mrs. Raleigh "to have a husband come back after seven years of sand." Mrs. Raleigh has borne the brunt of the household, and, Sian thinks, "the lady of the house oughtn't to do the bills. . . . It should be the gentleman" (93). It is indeed a shock to Mrs. Raleigh, who, when her spouse is presented to her, merely stares at him as if he were a stranger. It is unclear whether

Mrs. Raleigh is dumbstruck because she is so happy to be reunited with her husband or because she recognizes the impending loss of her independence, to which she has become so accustomed.

Her hesitation about how to greet her husband, understandable to contemporary readers, is resolved when Sian and her sister, Debbie, make Mrs. Raleigh kneel before her husband and the doll falls forward, landing at the captain's feet. This fall, unlike Curly's two falls, may or may not lead to happiness. Does Mrs. Raleigh fall in joy or despair at having her independence interrupted? Or did Sian push her, as is suggested? Is Rumer Godden's former ambivalence over any possibility of Laurence's return after his desertion reflected in this scene? Or does it reflect a fantasy of being cared for, since, as the story relates, the Captain will now defend his family?

Miss Charlotte's reaction to the reappearance of Thomas is much less complex than Mrs. Raleigh's response to her husband's return. Bertrand has asked his French cousin to send a sailor doll from her large collection because he feels guilty that Curly has been somewhat bruised at sea. The doll that arrives may or may not be the one taken away years ago, but the resemblance is close enough. The difference, interestingly, doesn't seem to matter (perhaps revealing Godden's attitude toward men at the time she wrote the story). As Debbie comments, "You can have another . . . fiancé," but you "can't have another father" (102). Miss Charlotte falls (dolls fall quite a lot in this story) into Thomas's arms and is, after a proper wedding, soon pregnant.

Bertrand returns Curly in time for the wedding, identifying the doll's home on seeing the celluloid Mrs. Lewis, whom Sian has optimistically hung on the door to lead Curly's rescuer home. Later, hearing that Miss Charlotte is pregnant, Curly wishes desperately for the baby to be a boy. The degree of pain he experiences at the thought that his wish may not be fulfilled may suggest the intensity of Rumer Godden's own childhood wish to be a boy or to have a brother, but it certainly communicates the horror of being forced to live falsely, to be locked inside oneself with no means of emotional expression. As the author observes, "When a doll is angry or hates anyone, there is nothing he—or she—can do." Unlike children, who can scowl, stick out their tongues, or seek other remedies, dolls, no matter "how much they suffer . . . have to be just the same, which perhaps is why dolls are so nice, but their feelings cannot help welling up inside them" (127).

Although Curly has up to this point been pictured as a cheerful doll, his pain may derive from his and/or Bertrand's sense of male vulnerability.

In this story, male dolls tend to get lost. Bertrand struggles to overcome his false self, and Sian's father is never mentioned. The birth of a boy doll symbolizes a wish for an authentic and ongoing sense of maleness.

Needles prick Curly's eyes, and he despairs as Morello quotes a "hateful rhyme about magpies":

One for sorrow
Two for joy,
Three for a girl
Four for a boy. (126)

Although Morello claims that she has seen three magpies, this omen is dismissed when twin boys are born and are given heroic seafaring names: Horatio Nelson and Frances Drake Raleigh. As the dolls' house becomes filled by boys, so Bertrand has entered into his full boy-nature, which includes the ability to communicate with girls through speech and silence. As Bertrand becomes friends with Sian and tells her about his own transformation from prig to real boy, communication between humans and humans and between humans and dolls is enhanced. Bertrand will teach Sian French, and she will teach him Welsh. Bertrand will then be able to converse with the Welsh Mrs. Lewis, whose silent presence led him to Sian; and Sian will be able to write to Bertrand's French cousin, who sent her the Thomas doll. When one member of the doll family observes that the denouement is very like a story in a book, the reader is jogged into remembering that this story, told from the dolls' perspective, is indeed a story in a book. It is a story that has much artifice—all of the coincidental fallings, findings, returnings—but it is a story whose theme is worthy of a book for children or adults: the universal journey from and back to the home of the self.

Both in mirroring aspects of the child's inner self and in reflecting the external world to the child, Godden's doll books provide children with miniature objects that help them to integrate inner and outer worlds, often under trying circumstances. As the Rustins observe in *Narratives of Love and Loss,* doll books, in general, can serve as projections of the child's inner life; conversely, in Kuznets's words, Godden's texts "resonate with conflicts beyond the projections or perceptions of the child characters" (114).

As has been noted and will become increasingly evident in the following chapters, child figures in Godden's nonjuvenile work are often hard pressed to find adequate vessels (helping figures, symbols) to contain the conflicts engendered by their exposure to overly agitating experiences. In *Kingfishers Catch Fire* and *The Greengage Summer,* for example, it remains moot whether children are more strengthened or undermined by failures of adult responsibility. Nevertheless, children in Godden's adult books often do find ways to draw on their own surprising resources. In so doing, they can provide models for adults, sometimes merely mirrors in which adults briefly view their own emotional and spiritual poverty. But if adults in Godden's books sometimes learn from children, what do children learn from adults?

Chapter Five

The Middle Years: Going Home? 1961–1969

In Godden's novels for children and adults of the 1960s, children and adults learn from one another "willy-nilly" (a favorite Godden term)—whether they wish to or not. In *China Court* (1961), children learn much from adults about the past and about the secret links that bind the generations and make all life interrelated. *China Court* can be seen as one more of the series of adult novels dealing with continuity within change that most notably includes *The Lady and the Unicorn, Take Three Tenses,* and *The River.* As the latest dip into the great river of time, it, too, shifts tenses, unpredictably bringing the childhoods of characters recently or long gone from the primary world to the fore at China Court, the old house that has contained generations of selves.

While the children who lived at China Court in past generations may have suffered misunderstanding and repression at the hands of their parents, a sense remains that their frustrated lives are fulfilled by future young protagonists who learn from their shadowy forebears' experiences. In *The Battle of the Villa Fiorita* (1963), children learn not about continuity between generations but about the sudden fragmentation of a family that can occur when the demands of motherhood and self are too much at odds. As two children attempt to rescue their mother from her film-director lover, for whom she's abandoned her family, they and their mother learn about the complexity of human emotions and relationships and about the ambiguous nature of art. If the world of art can be dangerously antisocial in the temptations it presents, it can, they learn, also expand the soul and help create a redeeming sense of selfhood and universal oneness despite apparent chaos.

If in *China Court* home represents integrity, in *The Battle of the Villa Fiorita* it represents self-annihilation. In *The Kitchen Madonna* (1967), the home and art are redemptive for the emotionally homeless middle-class boy whose baby-sitter, Marta, teaches him that home and religious reverence are at the center of the self. In crafting a religious icon for Marta, he not only finds a spiritual and possible professional home in art but teaches his busy parents that love, imagination, and spirituality should be priorities in the home.

China Court

China Court is a symbol of continuity and security, which, through Mrs. Quin's love, imagination, and religious reverence, will provide spiritual as well as physical sustenance for its heirs for generations to come. The book opens with the death of the widowed Mrs. Quin. As a child—the orphan Ripsie—she had come to live with the Quin family, and in time married a Quin son, inheriting China Court, which has served as home for Quins since 1840. The book is appended with a family tree, and the house resounds with voices from generations back, voices including those of the Ur-parents Eustace and Adza, their nine children, sons- and daughters-in-law, and Ripsie/Mrs. Quin herself. Also alive in the present (though all times seem present) are Mrs. Quin's granddaughter Tracy and her husband-to-be, Peter.

"Once upon a time," China Court was "like a nest,"[1] and Eustace, expanding on the bird metaphor, referred to his children (Mary, Eliza, Anne, Little Eustace, Mcleod, Marion, Lucy, Jared, and Damaris) as "the Brood." Jared had two sons with his embittered (because of his infidelity) wife, Lady Patrick. Ripsie, though in love with Borowis (who resembled his father, Jared, in reliability), married the more stable brother John Henry, with whom she had five children: Stace, Bella, and three daughters referred to only as "the Three Graces" because they resemble one another so closely in their clichéd, unimaginative behavior.

The novel has a fairy-tale quality; indeed, "once upon a time" could refer to any point in the novel. As Mrs. Quin retells stories about China Court's past to her granddaughter Tracy, she thinks they sound "like fairy-tales," for "stories, she knows, can never be really told, so much of them is hidden." It is "as if, with time, truth leaks out of them" (9). Yet only in the telling and retelling of stories, as in the multiple versions of stories in Godden's novels, can the truth possibly become clearer from a variety of perspectives.

China Court has "always been a halcyon place for children, but the only one of them who realizes this is Ripsie, because she is shut out" (113), like the abandoned third child in fairy tales. Small, lithe, and swarthy, like Lark of *Take Three Tenses,* of doubtful parentage (is Jared her father?), Ripsie as a child is taken in by Jared and Lady Patrick and becomes a playmate of their two sons. She is determined, proud, and passionate, although she is barely suffered by elders and servants and is a Cinderella-like figure, relegated to "the back stairs" (115). When Lady Patrick orders the removal of a small grotto Ripsie and a playmate have built by the road, Ripsie rebuilds and then tends it in a secret place "and the grotto grew into the garden" that now graces China Court. Indeed, this secret garden now revealed "was implicit in the house" (91); Lady Patrick has merely superimposed upon it. Her garden, Mrs. Quin observes later, "rescued her as a child" in "times when I didn't want to think, or could not bear to, in any emptiness, there was always the garden" (89).

Ripsie is not the only abandoned child in the book. Although Adza's and Eustace's children are well taken care of, they are in some ways neglected. Eustace makes out a Victorian timetable of lessons and activities ("To be called" 6:45, etc.) for his children that carries them from dawn to dusk and in a sense robs them of some of the halcyon days Ripsie enjoys despite her loneliness (58). Stolid and square in his frock coat, Eustace loves his children, but, like Adza, who "is even squarer than her husband" (60), he cannot nurture their imaginations.

Although Azda's children strike her as unusual (those "strange egret-like children that she has produced—not swans, egrets, those outlandish birds with coveted feathers" [81]), she has not a clue about their true natures, which will be expressed in increasingly eccentric ways as they mature. Jared will be unfaithful to his wife; Anne will become excessively religious; Damaris will be reluctant to marry and will die early; and Eliza, a girl of intelligence and ambition, will become increasingly frustrated by the limitations imposed on her as a female.

Eliza craves theater, gaiety, and knowledge. She grills her small brother on his visit to a claywork: "What is china clay? It is a high grade white or nearly white clay, formed by the natural decomposition of mineral feldspar" (63), she chants, echoing the tone of Mrs. Barbauld's *Lessons for Children* (1801). But Eustace will not take Eliza anywhere, and she knows "it is no use asking Papa either; he doesn't know or care—about *anything* . . . not about the hummingbirds in Mr. Gould's collection at the Zoological Society's Garden in Regent's Park; nor that it takes only eleven hours to get to Paris; nor about Mrs. Fanny Kemble's Shakespeare Readings; nor the agent of Mr. Hampton's balloon. He does not care a pin about any of them" (62). She asks Adza why father, rather than mother, reads prayers and is dissatisfied with the response, "It's Papa's place, dear." Her unceasing questions make her mother hear in her a "cuckoo voice," with which she "cannot compete" (64). Eliza is indeed a cuckoo, misplaced in this family and this time, and will yield to the popular meaning of the word when in later years she is seen hoarding books and muttering to a headstone in the cemetery.

But Eliza will save China Court for Mrs. Quin's descendents, beginning with Tracy. For despite the prohibition against her entering the family business or continuing her schooling, Eliza will add a new dimension to her life when Jeremy Baxter, the family accountant, teaches her the value of the lessons in old books and she begins secret reading with him. When her parents die, she takes on housekeeping chores, demands payment for her work, and, to augment the small amount her brother pays her, cleverly begins to steal from household monies. With her savings, she buys and secretes away fine books, and when Baxter dies, spends hours reading aloud at his graveside.

When Mrs. Quin dies, China Court is in jeopardy. Her children insist that the house be sold to save money. Only Tracy's father, Stace, who died in the war, had inherited some of Mrs. Quin's sensitivity and non-materialistic values. Earlier in the book, Mrs. Quin had lamented having lost her children to nursemaids, recalling the relentless voice of the nanny. "You will visit the nursery once a day, ma'am," and only "at my time," the nanny had said, and her "round-headed rosy baby" had disappeared, coming back "for a year or two as the enchanting small boy in the portrait in her room but in a moment," it seemed to Mrs. Quin, vanishing again to school, "the dreadful system that snatches little boys away from their mothers and turns them into bony objectionable small monsters" (75). Unlike Adza, Mrs. Quin sends the girls to boarding and finishing schools, but they seem unambitious and opt out of choosing careers. Clearly, she prefers and mourns Stace. Stace's daughter, Tracy, will inherit Mrs. Quin's imagination and home. It is appropriate that she finds the list of Eliza's purchases, which leads her to the discovery of her aunt's hidden store of books, books that, in China Court, serve as magical objects of fairy-tale power. The final treasure discovered is the precious *Book of the Hours,* which when sold provides enough money to save China Court.

Tracy is another abandoned child. Her father is dead, and her mother, Barbara, is an actress who moves Tracy from home to home, continent to continent. The only stability Tracy has ever known was in her early years at China Court with Mrs. Quin. When "Tracy is taken away," Mrs. Quin "comes to understand how legends have arisen round toys, for the old toys seem to be possessed by a life of their own" (113). As a child, Tracy "has a secret game . . . called Children," in which she imagines herself the mother of three children, "Big Boy, Big Girl and Little A," sometimes even adding China Court's ceramic figures to her brood. Tracy's children "are not left to be blown about by any wind; they are kept safe and 'firm.'" For Tracy and Mrs. Quin, to "keep" or be "firm" means "it will not be broken" (271). Here, the ceramic figures seem to fill for the child Tracy a containing function similar to that of Godden's dolls.

Tracy has not been "kept," or "held" with firmness until meeting Mrs. Quin. When "the real children" who come to tea with Tracy at China Court ask her who and where her parents are, she replies, "Gone" and that "grown-ups marry . . . then they get tired of each other and they all change over" (271). Mrs. Quin knows Tracy's secret sorrow and comforts her at night wordlessly, wondering, "Why couldn't they, Barbara and Stace, think of the child? Like a little fly, Tracy is brushed out of the way, blindly. Is it a wonder if she is maimed?" (272) She rejoices that "At least, Stace, I thought about you . . . I didn't harm you." That is, she has never told anyone that Stace's real father was Borowis (John Henry's unstable brother, who was Mrs. Quin's true love) or that John Henry had offered to marry her possibly knowing she was pregnant.

Now Mrs. Quin proves herself a true fairy godmother, continuing to hold China Court and Tracy "firm." When her will is read, Tracy learns not only that Mrs. Quin has left China Court and all its possessions to her but also that Mrs. Quin has provided her with a husband, Peter St. Omer, the tenant of Penbarrow, the family farm. Tracy will inherit only if she marries Peter, whom Mrs. Quin has befriended. Tracy and Peter are in fact drawn to each other and agree to marry to preserve the house, to honor Mrs. Quin, and to care for one another. While Mrs. Quin was unable to provide financial help, Tracy finds Eliza's books, the valuable *Bonnefoy Hours,* indeed right under Mrs. Quin's pillow. This *Book of the Hours* had sustained Mrs. Quin through much of her life, and now it will provide her heirs with financial as well as spiritual sustenance.

There is an odd note at the end of this novel. In fairy tales, the marriage's consummation is rarely documented before Cinderella and Sleeping Beauty go on to live happily ever after. Here, there is awkwardness, as, after the wedding, Tracy and Peter are left alone at China Court. Each gazes at the other endlessly around the fire. Finally, Peter says, "Tracy if you poke that fire again, I swear I shall hit you" (301). When the independent-minded Tracy pokes the fire, he does indeed strike her, and the room turns into a great Quarrelling Room.

During their argument Tracy stumbles and one of the household treasures, the "Pale Blue Girl," a ceramic figure that she had taken as one of her children, crashes to the floor. This stops their quarrel. "That's how we keep things," she cries. "I loved her ever since I was a little girl. She was ours now and I smashed her" (302). Tracy is astonished when Peter replies, "Thank God"; she understands, however, when he explains: "Yes, because we were nearly smashing everything" (303). Now he feels free to say what he could not express before and she to agree. "Just now I want you . . . we have to be married," and "I am going to touch you. Pay attention, Tracy, you are my wife and I am going to kiss you," and "stop dreaming." As Tracy melts into his arms, she thinks, we are "two halves of a whole" (303). Tracy, Peter suggests, must sacrifice what has been the life-supporting but childish container for her emotions, the doll (an externalization of her narcissism), for a real-life love object.

The novel skirts the genre of cheap romance here, and the reader may wonder if Godden perceives the gulf between men and women to be so wide that it must be bridged by violence. Does this scene reflect personal experience of male dominance and ultimate acceptance of its place? Or is it, as Bruno Bettelheim suggests in his discussion of "The Frog Prince," that each partner must wake the other from the dreams of childhood by a symbolic shattering?[2]

That this latter interpretation may be the closest to the truth is suggested by the book's fairy-tale ending, as all the characters disappear into the misty background of forever after (and before): "And now the stories seem like tales," Mrs. Quin muses when she is very old and tired. "Perhaps they don't matter . . . except to the people who lived through them. The stories are all different . . . yet all alike" (304).

The Battle of the Villa Fiorita

In *The Battle of the Villa Fiorita* the fairy-tale ending is negated. Like Hansel and Gretel, Caddie and Hugh are on their own, impelled on a journey of self-discovery motivated by abandonment and need. Like Gretel, Caddie will come to recognize a previously unknown strength, and like Hansel and Gretel crossing the lake, she and her brother will cross over the English Channel on their way home, their treasure (in this case their mother) in hand. But unlike the fairy tale's, this story's end is a dark one, with future happiness by no means assured. Rather, the gulf between men and women, temporarily suggested but overcome in *China Court,* has widened, seemingly irreparably, and the days that lie ahead suggest an unbearable barrenness.

Fanny Clavering, mother of seventeen-year-old Philippa, fifteen-year-old Hugh, and twelve-year-old Caddie, has left her husband to run off to

Italy with the handsome film director Rob Quillet. She has, it is revealed, come to feel constrained by her loving but straitlaced husband, Darrell (another Eustace), and limited by her children's needs. In traveling to the Villa Fiorita, the children have refused to accept the passive roles of victims. In answer to pitying adults who say in their hearing, "It's always the children who suffer most," Hugh tells Caddie, "I won't be a victim," and Caddie concurs, "Don't let's be. Let's go."[3] Through clever planning and sacrifice (they forge notes to their schools; sell Caddie's pony, Topaz; and do without food), they travel on their own to the small town of Malcesina, Italy, to surprise their mother and bring her home.

Set far away from the village, the aptly named Villa Fiorita, where their mother lives with Quillet, is surrounded by "hedges of scented whitethorn on either side" with the "longest fiercest thorns they had ever seen. The gates are iron-barred and high, the bars set close: obviously people are not meant to get in" (1). Is Fanny imprisoned or protected by the hedges? Is Quillet her captor? Does she await liberation from a temporary lapse in her true self? Or is he her liberating prince? Does Fanny resemble the caged wild birds whose prisons line the villa's wall, or the free "swallows nesting under the roof," flashing "dark blue and cream-coloured as they flew in and out"? (5). Everything, the reader will see, depends on perspective. But whatever perspective is in the end chosen, the tone is of a failed fairy tale. The villa, Godden tells us, "might have been anywhere; it was simply a place where two opposing forces were to meet, as two armies meet on foreign soil to fight a battle" (1).

On entering the villa, the children are struck by the strangeness of their mother's possessions, her new scent, called "non toccare," the ornate bed, and the sense of an intimate and provocative space they have invaded. Like Tracy, forced to leave China Court as a child, the children have themselves lost all sense of their own place or space, as their father has given up their old cottage for a flat in London, in which "the kitchen was the most homelike room," if "any of it could be called homelike" (21). So displaced are they that when an astonished Fanny finally greets them, they ask, "Are you Mrs. Quillet now or . . . Mother?" (34). The struggle over Fanny's identity is engaged. Rob and she are not yet married, and while Fanny does not tell them what to call her, she replies, "Children are always welcome, where their mother is. Always." This provokes Rob to respond, "It sounds false. . . . No one, however near and dear, is welcome at any time. . . . Be yourself, Fanny." And when Fanny counters, "I am myself. This is me," Rob has the audacity to respond, "It's not. It's a kind of play-acting" (48). Fanny is unsure of her identity, and she half shares Rob's sense that the heightened passions at the villa will allow her true self to emerge.

Rob seems to think of life as art, and, indeed, at the Villa Fiorita, as part of the battle, art constitutes a threat to the home and one's sense of place. Whereas in London the children perceive their kitchen as the only homelike room in the house, here Quillet takes over the kitchen table at the villa to do his writing. The very name of the film on which he is working, "Diamond Pipes" (referring to the process by which the heat at the earth's core forms subterranean pipes that solidify into blue clay, in which diamonds can be found), suggests the explosive nature of art, love, and the hidden self.

For Fanny, being a wife and mother meant one-sided sacrifice, contrasted with the housewife's dream she now lives of being wholly pampered. Motherhood, she thinks to herself, can "blot you out." Although Fanny privately acknowledges that "the moral books are right when they tell you, you are playing with fire, tasting goblin fruit" (86), her attempts to resist Rob have made Fanny feel as if she were "sleep-walking" (87), for, she thinks, "Being without Rob was like being put back to sleep when you had been awake" for the first time since childhood. The comparison to fairy tales is made clear: "What wisdom there is in the old fairy-tales . . . 'The Sleeping Beauty'—only I am not a beauty, thought Fanny and Rob did not even have to kiss me to shatter me awake; but the end of 'The Sleeping Beauty' was pure fantasy; in real life even the heroine has to go back to sleep'" (88). Indeed, the rambling, awkward phrasing of Fanny's lengthy thought-sentence suggests her somnambulent sense of her life before Rob entered it. Fanny's mental reversal of the happy ending of "The Sleeping Beauty" presages the novel's conclusion, in which a defeated Fanny returns home, her children's captive. As she had observed earlier, "Children bound one into a rule" (79), but the battle of the Villa Fiorita, which is ultimately an internal one, of Fanny's conflict between lust and duty, of her different perspectives on the self, continues throughout. For Fanny, "who had always been peaceful," seems, now that her children have arrived, "on jerk strings." She, "who had been almost selfless, 'willy-nilly,' she might have said, thought only of herself. 'I.' 'I.' 'I,'" struggling like a moth to break its chrysalis" (98).

In the course of the book, Caddie and Hugh also emerge "willy-nilly" from the chrysalis. For Godden, willing can be the key to achievement, growth, and happiness, but, as will be seen in *The Battle of the Villa Fiorita,* growth sometimes takes place while one is willing something else. Caddie and Hugh put all their willing into achieving their mother's return home. When Rob prepares to return the children to England, Hugh becomes sick, and his trip is delayed. Attempting to put Caddie on a plane by herself, Rob cannot help responding to the look on her face, for he "had seen that look before, on a famine child in India, doomed hopelessness" (160). Caddie rejects Rob's easy reassurances: "this all seems dreadful now, but it will be all right" (159–60), and openly tells him that her intention is to reclaim her mother. At the last moment, as though yielding to her will, Rob has her pulled from the plane and takes her back to the villa.

Rob, after all, wages his own internal battles and is capable of seeing things from a child's perspective. He is upset when passengers brush against her on line: "Can't they see she's only a child, and travelling alone? But Caddie was too old, and too young to arouse any interest." He likens her to all the sacrificial animals Caddie refuses to identify with, "a small bullock . . . driven down the ramp," her skeleton like "a lamb's bones" (161).

What Rob will offer Caddie next is not the sacrificial altar, or what she has come to the Villa Fiorita in search of, but something very different— experience. He takes her first to an elegant dinner and then to the Opera at La Scala. Caddie enters a new world in which she finally escapes herself. It was "as if a skin parted in her mind, something tight and stretched in which she had been sealed and against which her unhappiness had boiled and seethed. For days she had been too small a Caddie for all that was in her. 'I have grown too big for me,' she could have said." The music warms, surrounds, and frees her, so that she "seemed to be stroking Topaz's neck again . . . this singing vibrated and flowed through her so that she seemed to be stroking, not a pony, but life itself" (171).

As she temporarily forgets her one-sided goal of rescuing Fanny, Caddie feels like a bird "let out of its cage" and experiences "a oneness" in which "everything is everything" on "the tide of that singing." While this sense of integration lasts only a few minutes, Caddie feels that she has "laid her hand on truth, tried to grasp it and her hand was empty— but not quite empty, because she knew now it was there" (172). Caddie has been given an insight, a gift to which she may be able to return in the future.

Rob's gift to Caddie does not make her battle against him less intense. Indeed, Rob likens her to an "infant Hannibal," who "took a solemn oath he would never be at peace with the Romans." Rob recognizes that Caddie's arguments are "like elephants. They squash you flat" (182). "A cross," Caddie exclaims, "That's a funny thing to have hanging over your bed" (183). When Darrell finds it convenient to allow the children to remain in Italy an extra fortnight, Rob invites his own motherless daughter, Pia, to join them. In so doing, he unknowingly adds support to Hugh's and Caddie's cause, and he also complicates Hugh's one-sided perspective. Ten-year-old Pia is captivating, the opposite of the solid, unadorned Clavering children to whom she condescends. She, too, wishes to break up Fanny and Rob's union and initiates a hunger strike that helps the children win a major skirmish.

Rob and Pia present temptations to the Clavering children. Even while they struggle against the Quillets, their allure continues: "I wish Rob were my father," Caddie thinks to herself. The children are taken by the freedom of no set bedtime for Pia, who is "left remarkably free, almost as if she were grown up," and by Rob's playfulness when he is in the mood. "I want a child," he will call, and take them off on long romps where they are allowed to "taste everything." While Rob believes that children "should keep their places," he also believes they "should be free to grow up" (216). The sensuous environment of the villa begins to stir Hugh's manly feelings, as does the beautiful Pia. Hugh, like Caddie, admires Rob's physique, and is so moved by his mother's physical presence that he cannot bear to be touched by her. When Caddie asks Hugh, "What's fornication?" he orders her out of his room, thinking, "I must blink facts. . . . If I don't, I cannot bear them" (184).

Despite their wish not to let the children come between them, their disparate approaches to child rearing widen the gap between Fanny and Rob. When Rob spanks Pia, who had been on her hunger strike, Fanny says that force is "never fair," and "discipline shouldn't humiliate" (256). Rob retorts with disparaging remarks about the Clavering children's upbringing. When Fanny protests that "Pia never knows where she is" and that she is always dependent on Rob's whimsy, Rob replies, "She does. . . . She knows she has to study me and find out what mood I'm in. That will teach her to deal with other people" (215).

Caddie's next step is to visit a Catholic priest to seek his help in converting her mother to Catholicism, which she irrationally imagines will make Fanny return to Darrell. The priest takes her to the bus and, when he encounters Fanny and Rob, lectures them publicly about their sin. Rob is overcome with sadness and guilt, at spanking Pia, and at Caddie's pathetic face, and thinks: "Caddie . . . brought you into real truth, that little bungling ignorant girl and—they won the first day they came" (270).

Shortly thereafter, perhaps as a result of the guilt inspired in her by the priest, Fanny, who has been pregnant briefly, miscarries. For Fanny, as for so many Godden characters, gardens are steadying influences, but her efforts to calm herself by touching the trees in the garden are unsuccessful, and Fanny feels that her reality has been overturned. Fanny takes her loss as an omen and tells her children she is ready to go home with them. But this Fanny is different, a robot. She is relieved when Rob enters to announce he is taking her away, for "children cannot be allowed to dictate, or govern." Fanny, unable to make a choice, claims to be will-less. "You are kidnapping me," she tells Rob, and despite Rob's attempt to deny it, "I am not. . . You are coming, that is all" (279), she goes with him as though in a dream.

Caddie feels on the edge of complete loss, with "nothing and no one to hold on to. She would always be alone now." But now she makes a "startling discovery: she was alone, defeated, she had lost everything—and she was still herself, Caddie, still all right. Then it doesn't matter what happens to you. . . . You go on," she thinks. Caddie experiences moments of enormous growth, "as if a tight skin had parted in her mind." She sees herself as an "old, old" lady looking back "down the years" and has a sense of "steady rowing" (281). She is no longer an unconscious little girl: "I have known moments . . . though I'm still not twelve" (282), she thinks. Indeed, in her secret knowledge and sense of self despite loss, Caddie may now be richer in internal resources than her mother. Fanny seems as storm-tossed and vulnerable as the sailboat that capsizes, nearly drowning Hugh and Pia. When the two children are rescued and hospitalized, Rob and Fanny are isolated from each other in their concern for their own children. The children have separated them after all, and when Caddie later asks where Rob is, Fanny responds, "gone." The word rings like a bell through the last pages of the book. Hugh wants to see Rob; he is confused about his feelings about Pia, "this odd way that Pia had of making him do things better, be stronger than he was" (306). He concludes, "I don't understand anything." But Rob is "gone" because, as Caddie tells Hugh, "we have won after all" (307).

It is a bittersweet victory, for Pia is irrevocably gone, too, far away with Rob, and the Claverings must vacate the villa for the next tenants. Fanny has, she feels, suffered a terrible loss and almost paid the most terrible price, the loss of her son, for what she now sees as her wrongdoing with Rob. "If you do wrong, you will be punished, terribly punished." Yet her confusion is evident in her feeling that had her and Rob's baby been born, they would all have been safe, "as children do bind you" (310). But her three children have not bound her "safe" at home, nor would her "sin" be less had the baby lived. Underlying the contradiction between her wish to be saved by a baby and her knowledge that her children have not bound her safe is Fanny's suspicion that children will be punished for adults' sins; adults' irresponsibilities will make children into victims, and it is only grace and the courage of children that can save them.

Again, it is Rob who makes the decision to call Darrell. When the children lead Fanny to a waiting car, she is emotionally dead, catatonic— a nonentity. As they drive out the villa gate, the garden hedge scatters and the sharpness of the underlying thorns is revealed.

In *The Battle of the Villa Fiorita,* art is seductive and treacherous, as is love. The garden and house, Godden's most powerful images of stability, offer no escape from pain. Children are potential victims or tormentors and wardens. Fanny's life on returning to London is unimaginable. But the children have had a taste of experience, a glimpse into the future, that, while curtailing their childhood, has given them a foretaste of adult pleasures and pains. Caddie, and to a lesser extent Hugh, may have gained, along with a more complex perspective on life, a strong sense of initiative, self, and possibility that may serve them better than their mother's scant resources have served her.

The Kitchen Madonna

If *The Battle of the Villa Fiorita,* clearly a book for adults, concludes with a hopeless Fanny being led home, her best hope to become a "Mousewife" again, *The Kitchen Madonna,* a children's book, begins on a note of children's empathy for adults' unhappiness: "The children did not like it that Marta was unhappy."[4] Marta is the Polish maid who provides a warm heart and hearth and makes Gregory and Janet's home, particularly the kitchen, "inexpressibly lovely," more so, it seems, than their architect parents, who are often kept late at work.

As the Rustins point out in *Narratives of Love and Loss,* the name *Marta* conjures up "martyr" and "mater" (103). Marta has given up everything of her old life; she is a refugee, driven out of Poland, never to see her family or people again. Greg sets out to mend her losses, to heal the gap between images of fulfilled and unfulfilled mother figures that is writ so large in *The Battle of The Villa Fiorita,* where Fanny must be bereft no matter what her choice.

Perceived by his mother as self-involved and uncaring, Greg is really an emotionally abandoned child who can identify with Marta's sadness, for "he too sometimes felt that brooding unhappiness, especially at twi-

light, 'when Mother is still out,' he might have said, only he preferred to
keep that thought to himself" (10). Before Marta's arrival, their parents'
busy schedule has made Gregory and his sister feel like "incubi," always
being "fobbed off on people" (12). Greg, in particular, is tired of change,
and seeks a place, a core. Marta is a soul mate and senses this, telling the
children, "You have no 'good place'" (19). By this she means that they
have no communal warm kitchen where everyone sleeps together over
warmed bricks and, above all, no gorgeously emblazoned holy icon to fill
the empty spaces in the home and the heart. This icon of "Our Lady and
Holy Child" represents the core of the family, mother and child; as
Fanny says in *The Battle of Villa Fiorita:* children should always be welcome with their mother.

Greg feels a vast protectiveness for Marta and decides to get her an
icon for the kitchen so that she will be happy and not leave them. Like
Caddie and Hugh in *The Battle of the Villa Fiorita,* Greg, on his own, figures out complicated routes—in this instance, to the British Museum,
where he hopes to see an icon for Marta. He persuades Janet to give him
the money she has been saving for a pony: "Don't be selfish" (24), he
tells her, repeating his mother's words to him. Arriving at the icon room
of the museum, the children are disappointed to see the drab colors but
are told by an elderly connoisseur that "the bright colors are there
underneath . . . an icon is more than a painting. It is meant to be a link
between earth and heaven, a window opening onto sacred things" (27).

This description serves as a symbol for the buried self that Greg will
come to express through his search for and ultimate creation of and gift
to Marta of the Kitchen Madonna. Greg is known for his inwardness, for
he stores things inside. Although, as his mother says, "so much goes into
Greg and nothing ever comes out" (22), Greg loves to draw, to copy art
in museums; when the children finally discover a model of what they
want, he decides to make a copy of it for Marta, though he has never
made anything before. Janet remains supportive, and when Greg loses
hope because he has no money to buy materials for the icon, his sister
reminds him that he "can make it with think." Now Greg feels "as if
Janet had opened a little door in his mind, a door that had been shut,
and once again he glimpsed the picture" (52).

His creativity unleashed, Greg searches through ragbags, borrows cut-
tings from magazines, cuts into his favorite picture to gain a piece of blue
sky, and tries to pawn his expensive wristwatch to buy sparkling candy
papers for the frame. In the process of creating the icon, both children are
transformed, each sacrificing and each taking initiative. The Rustins

rightly include *The Kitchen Madonna* in their discussion of doll stories, for the icon Greg creates is, like the doll, like art itself, an externalization of his inner need for wholeness. Greg's transformation is most evident, but adults are transformed, too, becoming generous and childlike. When Greg tells the sweetshop lady why he wishes to pawn his watch, she says, "who would ever have thought you were that kind of a boy. Proper stuck-up I thought you were; never a word for anybody" (78), and gives him a multitude of candies for only an I.O.U. "Do you think," she asks, like a child herself, when "this wonder of a picture is finished, you could bring it and show it to me?" (80) The children are generous in their praise of each other, and their parents are moved to tears as they comment that it was "made by a boy with imagination and love" (82).

The entire family decides to present Marta with the icon together. Greg chooses a "good place" (86) to hang it, and Marta is transformed to joy as well: "Now Marta never unhappy, never no more!" (87). Marta shakes Greg's hand as if he were an adult, and, indeed, he is well on the way to becoming one, for he will go on to make more madonnas for others he cares about, such as the sweetshop lady and his mother: "I shall make dozens of madonnas . . . better and better . . . more and more beautiful," he tells Janet. And, he even dares to dream, "Probably some day some of them will go in the museum. . . . I might be as famous as Fabergé" (89). In *The Kitchen Madonna,* unlike *The Battle of the Villa Fiorita,* art is transforming, saving, communal. Greg has begun to envision himself as an artist, buoyed by the healthy narcissism required to keep creating.

The books discussed in this chapter focus on the home as a source of self-hood or self-negation, with children past or present at the center. Worth brief mention here are two other works published in 1968 and 1969, respectively. The first is a collection of stories first published as *Swans and Turtles* and then as *Gone: A Thread of Stories,* and the second is a novel, *In This House of Brede.* In these books, written for adults, children figure less centrally than in *China Court, The Battle of the Villa Fiorita,* or *The Kitchen Madonna* and their suffering is less redeemed through self-development, growth, or art.

To discuss the later of the two first, the house at the center of this novel is the convent to which Philippa Talbot, a successful business-woman, mysteriously retires from the world. One of the meanings of *Brede* is "childbearing," and although in writing this novel about nuns Godden professed to wish to write a book free of children, the absence of children is, in fact, at the center of the book. As the novel gradually reveals, Philippa's loss of her five-year-old son in an accident years before has led her to seek refuge in the House of Brede.

When Keith suffocated in a gold mine, Philippa blamed his nurse, but she had herself, like Sophie in *Kingfishers Catch Fire* and Fanny in *The Battle of the Villa Fiorita,* been self-absorbed while her child suffered, "never dreaming" anything could go wrong.[5] The gold nugget with which Philippa has been left (given to her by Keith's friend after his death) is the nugget of love between mother and child, which she will ultimately transform into love of the Mother Church, where she will find her true home and restored childhood.

If the absence of a child is at the center of *In This House of Brede,* the title of Godden's collection of stories, *Gone,* suggests a note that rings through many of her works of the 1960s. In *China Court,* when the child Tracy is asked where her parents are, she responds, "Gone," awakening empathy in Mrs. Quin, who longs to make her feel at home. In *The Battle of the Villa Fiorita,* Rob and Pia are, at the book's conclusion, irrevocably "gone." The stories in *Gone,* Godden notes in the preface, are each "founded on a moment of experience, felt or seen or touched, that has long since gone, but that has left a small sediment or shape behind."[6] Most of these stories revolve around painful experiences of Godden's childhood in which she and her sisters were separated from their parents, living unhappily with their aunts and suffering in a string of schools. In "Down under the Thames," Alice (Rumer) is terrorized by the potty and by her aunt, who forces her to restitch her embroidery again and again. In "The Little Fishes," two sisters, miserable at school in London, endure the contempt of a nun who refers to them as "scum" in the hearing of a priest. These stories are permeated by a sense of emptiness and spiritual homelessness. But in these two stories, at least, the child is vindicated. In "Down under the Thames," Alice flushes the hated embroidery down the loo; in "The Little Fishes," the priest orders the nun to apologize to the "little fishes," who are out of their medium, homeless, at school.

The stories in this collection amply illustrate that if the moment that causes the child pain is "gone," that moment can leave a lifelong mark in the delicate sediment of a child's mind. How fortunate if the child—like Rumer Godden, and like Gregory in *The Kitchen Madonna,* Emily in *Breakfast with the Nikolides* and so many other Godden child protagonists—survives to live a creative life and, in so doing, redeems absence through the presence (presents) of art.

Chapter Six

Enough or Too Much?
Seeking Balance, 1971–1979

Godden's books of the 1970s are focused on the child or young adult reader. In 1960, Godden had become a grandmother for the first time; in 1972, she won the Whitbread Prize for children's literature for *The Diddakoi*. She expressed increasing pleasure not only in writing for children but in presenting readings of poets such as Gerard Manley Hopkins and Dylan Thomas to interest children in poetry.

The children's books of the 1970s—including *The Old Woman Who Lived in a Vinegar Bottle* (1972); *The Diddakoi* (1972); *Mr. McFadden's Hallowe'en* (1975); Godden's novel for adolescents or young adults, *The Peacock Spring* (1975); *The Rocking Horse Secret* (1978); *and A Kindle of Kittens* (1979)—focus on the tension between wanting and getting, on the unseen boundaries between absence, enough, and too much, between emptiness, self-fulfillment, and excess. The young protagonists of these books often veer too far in one direction or another before they, like the leaden dolls that Godden refers to in *The River* and in her autobiographies, find their center.

In discussing the work of the 1970s, it seems useful to return for a moment to *An Episode of Sparrows,* which contains seeds that will germinate in different patterns in the children's books published twenty years later and which can be seen as a novel about gratified desire. Embedded in the book is the folktale of "The Old Woman Who Lived in a Vinegar Bottle," in which a poor old woman throws a small fish she had bought for dinner back into the river and is rewarded when the fish, gifted with magical powers, grants her an endless series of wishes. As the old woman's modest wishes burgeon excessively, the little fish tires of the old woman's demands and withdraws his gifts, leaving her poorer but wiser. Although this tale lacks a child protagonist, its inclusion as the first of Godden's children's books of the 1970s highlights the quest for a balance of dependence and independence that seems to underlie the work of this decade.

The Old Woman Who Lived in a Vinegar Bottle

In 1972, Godden published the story of *The Old Woman Who Lived in a Vinegar Bottle* as a picture book for young children, prefacing it with the explanation that it had been taken from an old folktale and had been recounted by her family on "hair-washing nights" for four generations.[1] In this charmingly retold tale, illustrated by Mairi Heddewick, Godden has added only one element, the woman's cat, who serves as companion and bellwether. The cat's increasing dissatisfaction with her mistress's grandiose new lifestyle signals to young readers that something is amiss and that another change in fortune may be in the offing.

By the time the obliging fish berates the old woman for her selfishness and reclaims his gifts, even the youngest reader may think her punishment well-deserved. Back in her vinegar bottle, however, the old woman is no longer bitter (only her excessiveness had led her to her "vinegary" personality). Recognizing her mistake, she returns to the riverside to summon the fish once again, this time to apologize and hesitantly ask if she might have an occasional hot meal for herself and her cat. This wish is fulfilled, and the story ends with the fish observing that he is very happy that the old woman's story has not had a sad ending.

The lesson, if there is one, seems to be that wanting can be dangerous, but that sometimes it is necessary to want too much to get what one needs. While one may go overboard, excess may be necessary to achieve self-regulation. As in *An Episode of Sparrows,* "wanting is the beginning of getting."

The Diddakoi

The idea that excessive wanting may precede getting is also at the heart of Godden's next book. *The Diddakoi* is the story of a young orphan, Kizzy, who is a "diddakoi," that is, partially Gypsy by heritage (her mother was Irish). Kizzy lives with her grandmother in a caravan, attending school only sporadically. That Kizzy is akin to Lovejoy in *Episode of Sparrows* is suggested by her surname, Lovell, as well as by her cocky, independent nature. Kizzy doesn't go to school until the townspeople find her out, and when she does, she is regarded as a curiosity. The story opens as the other children mock her with a song: "Diddakoi / Tinker / Tinkety-tink."[2]

When Kizzy's grandmother dies, the caravan is burned—by custom and by her grandmother's request—and Kizzy is alone, except for her beloved horse, Joe. Admiral Twiss, a wealthy old bachelor, who had allowed Kizzy's grandmother to camp on his land, takes her in, and Kizzy finds in the admiral's home a link to a possible new life. A portrait of the admiral's grandmother, who liked Gypsies, hangs over the fireplace; the grandmother's name was also Kezia—Kezia Cunningham—and Kizzy, who sleeps in the old woman's childhood room, takes her day and month of birth for her own (the schoolchildren had taunted her for not knowing her birthday).

When the town board deems it unsuitable for Kizzy to live in the admiral's womanless home, Kizzy, like Lovejoy, finds a protector in a wise and compassionate woman, Olivia Brooke, a former magistrate. Like other Godden characters (Lovejoy, Olivia Chesney, and Mrs. Quin) and like Godden herself, this Olivia is a gardener, her values tied to the earth and the cycle of the seasons. Although Miss Brooke is a single woman, she requests and—despite the objections of some village worthies—is given custody of Kizzy. An ex-barrister, Miss Brooke is not only a woman of the world but a nurturer with an intuitive understanding of children's needs. A great reader, she is an excellent role model for Kizzy, who grudgingly begins to respect Olivia Brooke, even while she often rejects her affection so as to maintain her own independence.

Resisting all who try to help her, Kizzy persists in antisocial behavior, flooding the floor with water from the shower, refusing to eat, and running away to the admiral. Each time, Miss Brooke responds with affection and understanding, attempting to nurture Kizzy without diminishing her independence. As she explains to Admiral Twiss, with whom she has developed a comradely relationship based on their caring for Kizzy, "I don't want an obedient child seething like a little cauldron underneath" (83). Miss Brooke wants Kizzy to live with her "of her own will." Recognizing that Kizzy's rebelliousness is rooted in her deepest wish—to cling to her identity as a Gypsy—she helps Kizzy fulfill this wish by giving her a present of a miniature Gypsy caravan, which, set in the garden, is big enough for two people to have tea in. When some schoolchildren attack Kizzy, falling on her like the herdschildren on Teresa in *Kingfishers Catch Fire,* Miss Brooke, unlike Sophie, is keeping watch nearby and saves Kizzy. Nevertheless, Miss Brooke understands that Kizzy must fight her own battles: "It's a children's war. Let the children settle it" (93).

As in *An Episode of Sparrows,* the protagonist's only friend her own age is a boy, Clem. His energy and honesty equal hers, and he protects her from the girls who mercilessly bully her. At one point, Kizzy is beaten so badly that she is bedridden for weeks and refuses to return to school. When she refuses an invitation to join the chastened children at a Guy Fawkes bonfire at school, Clem, horrified by Kizzy's threat to blow up the school and by her stubborn persistence in her role as outcast, persuades her to allow some of the girls to visit her at home. The children are enchanted by the caravan and take turns going inside to have tea with Kizzy, who, as she explains the Gypsy life to them, becomes more and more boastful. She pours petrol on the bonfire, asserting that she can make it "as big as I like" (124), and sets off an explosion that endangers the main house in which Miss Brooke is asleep upstairs. Tragedy is averted when Kizzy's main persecutor, Prue, shows her courage by orchestrating Miss Brooke's rescue, at great hazard to her own life.

Recognizing that her boasting, her excessive wanting, has almost killed Olivia, Kizzy, dazed, is reborn, wondering, "My wagon was burned, just like Gran's. Then am I dead?" Indeed, in a sense, "the old Kizzy was dead" (130). She achieves a new understanding that like Prue, who is complex, both bully and heroine, she herself can be both Gypsy and member of the society by which she now finds herself accepted. She is, she says, both "Kizzy and Kezia. Half and half" (138). Far from deserting her, the universal fish continues to shower gifts on Kizzy and all those about her. Alarmed by Olivia's brush with death, Admiral Twiss abandons his lengthy bachelorhood to propose that they marry and raise Kizzy together. Kizzy is given her first birthday party and, in honor of her inauguration into her new family, is given a name that embraces all aspects of her physical, mental, emotional, and spiritual being—"Kezia Lovell Cunningham Twiss."

As all of the schoolchildren arrive for her party, Kizzy learns that her caravan, the house of the Gypsy self, has not been destroyed, only damaged. The children have refurbished it and lead it into the garden behind a pony that Admiral Twiss has gotten to replace her old horse, Joe, who has died. In the end, all losses have been restored, and the onetime pariah is integrated into society, to the benefit of all. The story ends as it began, with schoolchildren singing the Diddakoi song with which they had once taunted Kizzy. This time, though, it is sung by new students who admire Kizzy and romantically wish to be Gypsies themselves.

Mr. McFadden's Hallowe'en

Mr. McFadden's Hallowe'en is also a children's book about the integration of an outcast into society. If in *The Diddakoi,* however, it is adults like the admiral and Miss Brooke who help to integrate a child, in this book, set in rural Scotland, it is two children who effect the entry of an old curmudgeon into the social scheme.

Eight-year-old Selina is the family "outcast" because of her mischievous, untrammeled nature. Sometimes given to rages and often clumsy, she is one of Godden's cocky, independent girls. Like Lovejoy and Kizzy, she is best friends with a boy, the orphan Tim, who lives with his abusive aunt and uncle. When Selina's great-aunt Emily dies, she leaves the village £20,000 to build a park to benefit the entire community, but it cannot be built because Mr. McFadden, the town's biggest landowner, refuses to sell the necessary land. On her ride through the countryside, Selina meets Mr. McFadden himself and witnesses his meanness when he allows his big goose to frighten her. Nevertheless, when she later finds the old man injured (a boulder has pinned his leg down), Selina makes use of her Brownie knowledge to dislodge the stone, help him onto her horse, and take him to his farm. Selina returns to the farm daily to help him, and, when she tells him about how Tim is abused at home, he permits her to bring Tim to visit.

Thus begins a relationship in which Mr. McFadden gradually reveals something of his past to the children. Urging Tim to go to school, he tells him that he himself had no choice as a boy but was forced to work on the farm rather than get an education. An orphan, Mr. McFadden had a dismal childhood, wanting in every way; but worst of all, as far as Selina is concerned, Mr. McFadden—like Tim—has never celebrated Hallowe'en. Selina determines to be a "good witch" and bring Hallowe'en to Tim and Mr. McFadden. As Mr. McFadden shares more of himself with the children, his heart is gradually softened, a process that will, in time, turn out to be beneficial not only to him but to the children and the entire town as well.

Meanwhile, the townspeople are angry at Mr. McFadden. The townschildren throw stones at Selina and try to burn down Mr. McFadden's home. Mr. McFadden is rescued a second time at the hands of a child when Tim warns him and saves the house. When the old man finds Selina tied to a tree by the same gang of children (as in *Kingfishers Catch Fire* and *The Diddakoi,* groups of children can be vicious to one another) and carries her all the way back to his farm despite his bad foot, he, like Selina and Tim before him, has the opportunity to prove himself a hero.

In Selina's saddlebag, Mr. McFadden finds sacks of candy and treats destined, he learns, for his Hallowe'en, because, Selina explains, "You

have never . . . had any Hallowe'en . . . nor anything nice; no wonder
you're so nasty." Selina has achieved her aim of making a "nice p-persson
from a g-gurney-faced old scunner"[3] (Mr. McFadden accepts this judgment of his character as accurate.) As a result of Selina's initiative, both
she and Mr. McFadden have been transformed: Selina has achieved her
goal of proving herself capable of being "a good witch"; Mr. McFadden,
having gotten what he "wanted" (in both senses of the word)—attention,
affection, and fun—is now willing to give up part of his property to the
town, to move from the personal confines of his isolated life to the communal. "Full content" (127) for the first time in his life, Mr. McFadden
adopts Tim and is affectionately accepted by the townspeople. For her
part in Mr. McFadden's conversion, Selina has earned the respect of the
community. Fittingly, the park and its gardens, representing unity, open
on Hallowe'en, for all ghosts of unhappiness have been buried, and young
and old have been mutually redeemed.

The Peacock Spring

With its complex examination of the wants and loves of Sir Edward
Gwithiam and his two daughters, *The Peacock Spring* is by far Godden's
most sophisticated book for young people. In *The Peacock Spring,* all of
the central characters are in some way outsiders in their environments
and all are possessed by overpowering wants. In the process of attempting to satisfy these wants, children are used by adults and, in turn, adults
by children, so that everyone seems caught in a tangle of dangerous
excess. In the end, some things are learned and some things gained, but
not necessarily what was wanted.

As in so many of Godden's novels, the image of the garden is central,
and the book begins with the Indian gardener and his mysterious well-
bred assistant planting flowers at the United Nations House in India,
where Sir Edward, the English representative, awaits the arrival of his
daughters from England. Una, the eldest, is reserved, somewhat plain,
brilliant, and ironic. She had been preparing for mathematics exams and
the university. Halcyon is the daughter of Sir Edward's second wife and,
with her carefree nature and pretty face, lives up to her name. The girls
have abruptly been summoned from their English school to India, osten-
sibly to keep their father company in his lonely position and to study
with Miss Lamont. But, as they learn not long after arrival, they are really there to serve as a cover for their father's affair with the governess. In
the course of the story, both girls, but in particular Una, who is the focus

of the book, learn not only about the true nature of their father's relationship with Miss Lamont but about appearance and reality, human nature and its limitations, and about cruelty and love.

The Eurasian Alix (Allie) Lamont is, as Una quickly discovers, a sham as a governess, who can only give her dictation from outdated children's texts. She becomes enraged when asked for help with the mathematics Una requires to prepare for the university. When Halcyon (Hal) asks Una why she can't try to get along with Alix rather than confront her with her lies, Una replies that she must be honest. While Hal is able to say that Alix's relationship with their father is not their concern, Una, whose name suggests truth (and whose bluntness is reminiscent of Kizzy's and Lovejoy's), insists on bringing into the open the fact that their father has misused them by hiring Alix as a governess to mask her real role as his lover and to gratify his own desires.

Unwilling to accept that only Edward and Alix, the adult world, can will desire into reality, Una thinks of the ninepin doll she had been given as a child in India—"so small it had fitted into a matchbox but, cast in metal, it was weighted so that if it were knocked over, at once, or slowly, depending on the hardness of the knock, it stood upright again." This doll, "made to be knocked over" and "stand up again," is an apt metaphor for Una in her will to succeed, to prepare for the university, despite getting no help from Alix. Although the doll has been lost on their travels, it was as if it "sent her a message."[4] Opening her discarded math book (she had thrown it out the window in despair), she finds a mysterious peacock feather in it and, strangely comforted, begins the tedious task of solitary study in the garden. Just when she feels defeated, the handsome assistant gardener approaches to explain that it is he who left the feather in the book, for the peacock, while a symbol of bad luck in England, is an emblem of India and is sacred there.

The peacock becomes an emblem not only of India but of the passionate young love that springs up between Ravi and Una as Ravi (whose name suggests "ravishment" and whose good looks and apparent kindness bring to mind Eliot in *The Greengage Summer* and Rob Quillet in *The Battle of the Villa Fiorita*) helps Una prepare for the exams. Ravi reveals himself to be a highborn youth who has had to go into hiding because of his radical political activities. He is also a poet, and, during secret evenings in the garden, Una reads Ravi's poetry aloud from an unlined book bound in a red cotton cover. The book, which appeals to Una's secretive self, seems to serve the same purpose for Una that the garden in *An Episode of Sparrows* does for Lovejoy—it is a vehicle by which she begins to define her own identity, here in terms of the vast otherness of India itself. Una admires Ravi's poems because "they were plain and spoke of plain, intrinsic and indigenous Indian things." Plainness takes on new meaning, and when Una asks Ravi if she is herself "very plain," his response implies that she is like the India of his poetry—indigenous to herself (112).

Although Ravi helps her appreciate her true self, as Una lives an increasingly double life, forced to lie to her father and Alix about her whereabouts, she also learns about duplicity and loses the "oneness" her name implies—a oneness of vision that sees things unadorned and speaks the truth despite the consequences. Because she and Hal might be sent back to England if Alix were dismissed, Una even begins to protect Alix by coming to her defense and lying when it appears that her father may learn about Alix's past or present inadequacies. Hal, however, is completely disillusioned when she witnesses Alix's meanness to her half-caste mother, whom she has sequestered from Edward and the girls. Bursting into tears, Hal, who has a crush on Vikram, a young Indian nobleman (who is himself in love with Alix), refuses to stop when Una warns that "Vikram will see you with red eyes and a swollen nose." "If Vikram is going to marry me," Hal responds, "he had better see me as ugly as possible." Una is filled with admiration for Hal's willingness and ability to be "plain" despite her beauty, to reject Alix's superficial graces. At the same time, however, she recognizes that the gap between her and her younger sister is more than two years—"'It's difficult for you to understand . . . you are only twelve,' thought Una. 'You haven't had time to be stained . . . you have nothing to hide'" (132).

Una's lesson that truth is complex is to be driven home more tragically through Ravi's betrayal of her. Ravi has been preparing for an important poetry contest, which he plans to win. He believes that with this honor to bolster him, he will ask for and be granted Una's hand in marriage, despite the gap between their two cultures. But when Una becomes pregnant, they flee to the countryside, Una dressed in Indian garb, and hide at his grandmother's home (Ravi's parents will not accept them any more than Una's father would). Despite Ravi's romantic quotation about childbirth from *The Upanishads*—"In the fire, the gods find the offering: from the offering springs the child" (176)—when Sir Edward pursues the lovers with the police, who offer Ravi his freedom and the chance to enter the contest if he abandons Una, Ravi succumbs to self-interest. When Una realizes Ravi is not going to join her in a last opportunity to flee, she asks, "You don't want to come?" Ravi rejoins,

"Want—not want—that is not the question. The fact is . . . I want to read my poems" (235). Una also learns that Ravi is hiding from the police for an assault he committed as a student. If Una has seen Ravi as a peacock, she now knows why "the peacock gives those terrible screams." He "has looked down and suddenly seen his feet. He had been so busy admiring his train that he had forgotten he had them" (frontispiece). Una, who is trundled home to face a forced abortion the next day, finds an unexpected ally in Alix, who pleads with Edward to be merciful to Una, arguing that her own mother would regard abortion as a sin. In defending her mother when Edward sneers at her "mumbo-jumbo," Alix has also come to terms with who she herself is and has integrated the wisdom that had been an outcast but essential part of her being: "Mumbo-jumbo is what you hear from outside and do not believe. What you feel in you is true" (244). That the road toward wisdom is a long one made up of many struggles of the kind Alix and Una have undergone is suggested by the image of Ravi's grandmother. In the final stage of life, she wears no jewelry—her nose and ear holes are empty—and she radiates a peace before which "Edward's urgent importances seemed to dwindle into perspective because this was not a willed peace, a shutting away, but peace itself, steady, kind, unruffled" (229).

Una is only at the beginning of the long journey toward this peace. Although she tries to excuse Ravi, allowing the importance of art over life, one senses that this answer is not satisfactory, as Una feels on her leg "an infinitesimal Ganges, but of blood: not heart's blood but womb blood which, for a woman, is far deeper" (250). The miscarriage in which she loses the fetus is also one in which her innocence dies. She and Hal are sent back to school in England to get on with their lives and assimilate their experiences as best they can: Una to conjecture whether men and women are indeed like the pair of dressed-up monkeys she had been repulsed by in a temple courtyard, circling around each other in a sexual frenzy, manipulated by their laughing keeper. Whether Sir Edward and Alix will go on to build a new life based on a deeper and more honest understanding is left an open question.

As in *The Diddakoi* and *The Old Woman Who Lived in a Vinegar Bottle*, *The Peacock Spring* ends as it began, in a garden, with the gardener and Ravi's successor planting anew as they await the arrival of the house's new sahib. In the words of *Ecclesiastes*, there is "a time to plant, and a time to pluck up that which is planted," and this undying need cannot be shunted aside despite human suffering and dissatisfactions. Whether human needs have been fulfilled as desired or not, growth has taken place in the gardens that are Godden's novels (Una likens flowers to words); none of the central characters in Godden's novels remain the same, and although *The Peacock Spring* ends with the death of a potential child, if there is, as *Ecclesiastes* observes, "a time to kill," the cycle of life suggested by the concluding image of the garden suggests that following their Peacock spring, Una, Hal, Alix, and Edward may yet find a "time to heal."

The Rocking Horse Secret

The next book for children on Godden's roster is *The Rocking Horse Secret*. This book shares with *Mr. McFadden's Hallowe'en* the theme of very young and very old coming together in a helping relationship in which deeply held wants are filled. Tibby, a much milder version of Godden's other girl children, nevertheless feels rebellious when her mother, the housemaid, forbids her to play in the nursery of the old house in which Miss Pomeroy, a senile old woman she has never seen, lives a secluded life. Tibby finds in the nursery an ancient rocking horse she names Noble and is sometimes surprised to find the horse rocking gently when she arrives.

Once, while Tibby is riding Noble, Miss Pomeroy, for whom time has stopped, appears and teaches her a lively hunting song she used to sing to Noble as a child. Tibby, Miss Pomeroy informs her, was named after her, Tabitha, but does not live up to her in courage: "I hate nicketty picketty riders," she says. "I'm not nicketty picketty," Tibby replies, "I'd ride Nobel hard—if I could." Miss Pomeroy helps Tibby overcome her shyness and obedience by urging her to "ride Noble as hard as you like, when you like,"[5] despite the adjurations of her mother and Jed, the young caretaker. In turn, Tibby helps Miss Pomeroy enjoy her second childhood. Warning Tibby not to become one of those apparently "nice little girls . . . Nimini-pimini" (33) types like Miss Pomeroy's own two sisters, the old woman promises Noble to Tibby, writing her deed on a piece of paper, which Tibby hides in a hole under the horse's tail.

When Miss Pomeroy dies, her "Nimini-pimini" sisters (who are definitely *not* nice) appear and try to take over the house, ejecting Tibby, her mother, and Jed. Tibby, however, who has integrated Miss Pomeroy's teachings, knows where the will is hidden—in the same place Tibby has hidden the deed for Noble. Emboldened, when the sisters come to sell Noble and declare the house theirs, Tibby runs away to find Jed, who helps protect Tibby and her mother while they reveal the will's contents.

Miss Pomeroy's "will" is that Jed inherit the house. Miss Pomeroy will get what she wanted—her house will not go to her nasty sisters but will be home to Jed, Tibby, and her mother. More than that, Miss Pomeroy has succeeded in passing on her secret strength to her namesake Tibby.

A Kindle of Kittens

In contrast to *The Peacock Spring,* which ends with the loss of a child, the children's book *A Kindle of Kittens* (1979) focuses on birth and on the ability of the female—albeit a cat—to survive on her own.

Cat is homeless, but a number of people leave food for her, including the neighborhood poet, who in calling her "my wishful fishful sprite"[6] suggests a connection between the stray cat; the patient, universal fish of *An Episode of Sparrows* and *The Old Woman Who Lived in a Vinegar Bottle;* and the muse of inspiration, who (at least in Godden's case) never seems to weary.

When Cat meets a Tom who introduces himself as "He-Cat," she begins to define herself in terms of him: "Then . . . I am She-Cat." Soon she bears her kindle in a "broken greenhouse among flowerpots." The kittens grow in their dilapidated nursery, and their names assert their identity as well as aspects of their mother, who has kindled them: Funny (humor), Sunny (warmth), Money (elegance), and Honey (sweetness and creativity).

He-Cat disappears and She-Cat decides that she must find an appropriate home for each kitten. Plodding through the town, investigating houses until "the pads of her paws were sore," She-Cat is in her determination reminiscent of Godden in her role as a single parent and in her prescription for the writer, who requires "constant work, day and night" ("Will to Write," 13) to accomplish her aims. Finally, She-Cat makes her wish come true. Funny is matched with the Town-crier—one's cry echoes the other's; Sunny is left for the quiet old woman who "needs a little sun in those dark rooms"; Money goes to the neighborhood mansion, and Honey is left to the poet.

She-Cat has kindled life, not only for herself but for others in the community. In the end, however, when He-Cat calls to her again, she "shut her ears," for "she could stick one leg high up in the air now." Like Godden and her protagonists, She-Cat remains, in the last analysis, cocky and independent, ultimately refusing to be defined by anyone else, even her creator.

In the books Godden wrote for children and young adults in the 1970s, it appears that to achieve balance, it is sometimes first necessary to want and get excessively. The old woman who lived in a vinegar bottle and Kizzy want too much but are pulled back to the center by the natural consequences of their actions, which, fortunately, they survive. Unlike Lovejoy, who finds support in her garden and in friendship, one senses that Kizzy could not have achieved balance without Olivia Brooke and Admiral Twiss. Although Mr. McFadden, as a cynical adult, has stopped consciously wanting/wishing, the underlying wanting/needing of his unsatisfied childhood has prevented him from being a decent human being. Only when the child in him can be given to him fully (by a child) can he take on his adult responsibilities and give freely to others. Child and adult help each other get what they want in *The Rocking Horse Secret,* too, where Miss Pomeroy teaches her shy namesake to desire and ride more fiercely, and Tibby carries out Miss Pomeroy's "will" that the old lady's abusive sisters not triumph.

Far more complexly, *The Peacock Spring* explores the tangle of wants in which Sir Edward Gwithiam's family is trapped, ending on a note of disillusionment symbolized by Una's miscarriage. Yet Una has grown through experience, and will in time, one suspects, move carefully on to more loving relationships. One senses at the end of *The Peacock Spring,* and more obviously in *A Kindle of Kittens,* an increasing emphasis on the durability, independence, and centrality of the female figure, an emphasis that will be underscored in the early work of the next decade.

Chapter Seven

The Long Road Home: Finding Integrity, 1981–1993

Books Rumer Godden wrote for children or young adults and published in the 1980s and 1990s include *The Dragon of Og* (1981), *The Valiant Chatti-Maker* (1983), *Thursday's Children* (1984), *Fu-Dog* (1989), *Listen to the Nightingale* (1992), and *Great Grandfather's House* (1993). The themes of these books are diverse; but, keeping pace with the century, each shows a progressive focus on the clearly achieved entry of its protagonist into his or her own house of the self.

In *The Dragon of Og,* a young dragon comes into his own with the help of a surrogate mother; the Chatti-Maker (pot maker) is also empowered (but subsequently weakened) by a strong woman—his Clever Little Wife; in *Fu-Dog,* an insecure little Chinese girl learns to accept all parts of herself with the help of a toy dog and her ancient great-uncle; and, in *Great Grandfather's House,* an overly confident little Japanese girl learns to temper herself and achieve self-integration with the help of a young boy and her great-grandfather. Finally, in the two balletic books for children of this period, *Thursday's Children* and *Listen to the Nightingale,* a young boy and girl respectively enter into the house of the self through the nobility of dance. In each of these books (except for the ambivalent *Chatti-Maker,* which, because it is child-free, will not be discussed here), the child or young adult achieves unambiguous integrity and is well on the way to living fully in all the rooms of the self.

The Dragon of Og

Following through on the fairy-tale aura characteristic of many of Godden's books of the 1970s and 1980s, *The Dragon of Og* opens with, "It happened long ago,"[1] when men and dragons fought each other in the lowlands of Scotland. In those days, the dragon was born in a dark cave below the wide river known as the "Water of Milk." While female dragons, we learn, are nurturing, he-dragons are not; they spend most of their time fighting with each other in the air, the winner descending to mate with his love so fiercely that he often kills the she-dragon.

Like She-Cat in *A Kindle of Kittens,* the mother of the young dragon is a survivor; she can take he-dragons or leave them. She finds a nest safe from the Father Dragon her son will never know. Before leaving her teenage son to fend for himself in the milky river (she is pregnant again and must find a nest for her new baby), she warns him not to alarm the neighboring people and not to emulate his uncle, who is something of a rake and a flamethrower who devours young girls.

His sexuality aroused by his uncle's stories and the sight of the village girls, the young dragon asks his mother if it would offend the villagers if he ate just one of their daughters "now and then," and is disappointed when she replies, "I believe it would . . . so don't" (8). In an effort to integrate his mother's value system, the dragon curbs his appetite and chooses to live in the Water of Milk rather than in the caves where the male dragons congregate.

The young dragon lives gently and innocently by himself, not even retaliating when the village children throw pebbles, his only indulgence an occasional bullock snatched up in his great claws and swallowed in one huge gulp. When the dragon reaches young adulthood (900 years), however, a change takes place in the village—the last Lord of Tudergarth dies and Angus Og is declared chieftain. Like the male dragons, Angus has to fight the other chieftains to maintain power and is, by nature, warlike. Indeed, as Angus, his men-at-arms, and his warhorses cross the Water of Milk, it turns murky and smelly.

In contrast to Angus, his young wife, Matilda, represents a civilizing force. Although she is so delicate that the warlords wonder if she can ever bear a child, she is determined in her opinions and desires (like the dragon's mother) and begins to fix up the gloomy castle she and Angus have inherited, cleaning the "midden," or animal manure, out of its central court and hanging warming tapestries on the walls. So strange is Matilda to the villagers that all call her "She" rather than by name. In so doing, they unwittingly bestow on her her salient trait—womanhood, with its humanizing energy. "'She will not let her Lord walk into the great hall in his miry boots,' they said, wishing they could make their men do likewise" (19). Matilda exerts her influence not only on the home but on nature itself. Cultivating the garden and walking slowly along the riverbank, she listens to the birds and flowers, engaged in what seems to be "nothing"; she is not idle, however, as the villagers believe, but in a state of meditation in which she is at one with her surroundings. She is in fact so much at ease that when she encounters the sleeping dragon, she is able to acknowledge him, unafraid, as a soul mate ("Her eyes were as green as his own") and speak to him "in dragon language that has no sound" (22).

As the dragon and Matilda become fast friends, Matilda gives him nosegays and he, in turn, becomes less shy and increasingly frisky, blowing her skirts over her head with his dragon's breath. This fairy-tale romance of Beauty and the Beast is soon, however, to be overcast by trouble with Angus, who, accusing the dragon of devouring too many bullocks, uses him to distract the villagers from his own tyranny. Despite Matilda's protests, Angus, who has visions of becoming a greater noble than King David, insists on turning the dragon into an "it"—a fearful object, a mythical monster: "At first I thought I had taken too much wine, but no; I saw it spread its wings and this great shape came down, its eyes like green lamps" (28).

Angus sets out to slay the dragon, tricking him with a tempting "stick cake" filled with pitch (a traditional way of catching dragons); the dragon's mouth will stick shut, and if he attempts to breathe flames, he'll explode. Despite Matilda's warning, the dragon licks the cake and his tongue sticks to the roof of his mouth. The village children greedily devour the rest of the cake and an unnatural silence settles on the village of Og, to be lifted only when Matilda suggests that mothers use willow twigs to brush away the gluey pitch (in the process, suggests Godden in this embedded *pourquoi* tale, inventing the toothbrush in Scotland).

If Matilda is a protector and nurturer, she is also an integrator, accepting and helping others to accept all aspects of their being. After coaxing the dragon into the sun so that the pitch on his tongue can melt, Matilda is amazed and delighted when the dragon, hurt and angry at being treated unkindly, begins to flame. When she warns him that he may explode because of the pitch in his belly, he replies, "I'll show them explode!" Though Matilda lays a hand on his head to calm him, she remarks, "Splendid" and "I'm glad you have learnt to flame" (34). Thus, like a good mother, she accepts and regulates his anger so that he may master it and use it most effectively.

The dragon's ire increases as Angus drives herds of cattle far away from the river, and as the dragon's flames increase (he's been practicing), the Water of Milk boils up, poaching all the fish. The starving villagers are fed and bless the dragon; in contrast to Angus with his cake, the dragon has provided true rather than false nourishment. Angus, needless to say, is enraged at the loss of his fishing ground and declares that he will slay the dragon. No St. George himself, Angus takes Matilda's suggestion that he send Robert LeDouce to do the task. Matilda seems to intuit that the dragon must die in the form of his old self in order to be reborn in the form of an integrated self. As the gentle dragon hesitates to do him harm, Robert dispatches the creature easily, throwing the severed parts into the Water of Milk.

But when Angus reneges on his promise of payment, Robert, refusing to haggle, returns to the milky river and rejoins the severed parts, praying over the restored body. When Matilda, heartbroken, finally returns to the river, she finds a weak but reborn dragon in the milk of regeneration. Unlike his birth mother, who had warned him against flaming, Matilda informs the gentle dragon that he should have fought Robert LeDouce, "belched your flames at him and sizzled him in his armour" (50). Returning to the castle, she asserts the supremacy of the female, preparing tubs of healing junket for the dragon and warning Angus that if there is any more killing, she will go back to her mother's house.

As a result of the abuse he has undergone, the dragon suffers from low self-esteem: "I thought I was a Dragon and I'm only a worm" (52), whose two pieces have been joined together, he laments to Matilda. Comparing himself to a worm, which despite its ability to regenerate when cut into pieces is the lowliest of creatures, the dragon concludes, "I don't feel like living." Evoking echoes of William Blake's *Book of Thel,* Matilda responds: "Don't you dare despise a worm. . . . It was by the power of the worm in you that you could join up and live" (53). Thus, all aspects of the self are necessary for true dragonhood.

After nurturing him on baby food, Matilda introduces the dragon to more bracing mead, and he awakens from a deep sleep much recovered. Back on his feed, the dragon requests bullock, and Matilda, hoping to avoid further conflict with Angus, makes a temporary vegetarian of the dragon by persuading him that since bullocks are vegetarian, eating barley and grass directly is the very same thing as eating bullock. Soon, however, the nation has been emptied of fish, eggs, barley, and grass; and Angus, who is unwilling to alienate Matilda further, gives in when she challenges him to "do something new . . . something an Og seems never able to have done. . . . Make peace" (59). Thus, Matilda's civilizing power has its effect on Angus as well as on the dragon, and, as a result, the dragon is permitted one bullock a month.

The dragon has been able to strengthen the feminine side of his nature and to resist the negative aspect of masculinity, represented in Matilda's narcissistic husband, Angus, who attempts first to reify and then to kill the dragon. Angus appeals to Og's greed, tempting him with the false food of the stick cake, like the witch in "Hansel and Gretel." In *The Dragon of Og*, the adolescent protagonist finds both masculine and feminine images on which to model his desires and actions. With Matilda's help, he can allow himself to be dissolved, or made vulnerable, in the Water of Milk by Robert LeDouce, who, as his surname signifies, is gentle as well as strong, and to be nurtured by the good mother, Matilda, until his appetites are regulated and he has fully accepted and integrated all the parts of his nature.

Hidden in the ever-nurturing Water of Milk, the dragon lives on, having achieved the integration of full dragonhood in a state of organized innocence. Thanks to the powers of Matilda (and Rumer Godden), the dragon outlives Angus, Matilda, their children, and their kingdom to become a legend in his own and all future times. Living eternally, he remembers all and is remembered by all through the power of the fairy tale.

Thursday's Children

Like *The Dragon of Og, Thursday's Children* is about bringing the component parts of oneself together. As in *A Candle for St. Jude,* the setting is balletic, but here the focus has shifted from an elderly ballet teacher to the brother and sister Doone and Crystal Penny of Pilgrim's Green, London. Their father is a greengrocer and their mother an ex-chorus girl with a lifelong yearning to be a ballerina. Her hopes have been projected onto her only daughter, who in her fair, pretty looks and shallow personality is reminiscent of Caroline in *A Candle for St. Jude.* Crystal takes ballet classes at the Empire Rooms with Madame Tamara, a less exalted dancer than Madame Holbein of *A Candle for St. Jude* (it will turn out later that Madame Tamara is not even Russian). Doone, the youngest of four boys, is dark and Gypsy-like in appearance. He is virtually ignored by his parents, especially his mother, who, like Griselda in *Take Three Tenses,* is furious at having so many children imposed on her by her husband. Consigned to sleep in the tiny ventilator room, designated an "unsatisfactory child,"[2] Doone takes refuge with his father's assistant, Beppo, a former circus clown who is the only one who seems to love him. Beppo teaches Doone acrobatics, and together with what he picks up when he sometimes accompanies Crystal to the Empire Rooms, Doone begins to develop his innate talents as a dancer.

Madame Tamara, far more tired and defeated than Madame Holbein, is frightened of her students' mothers, especially of Mrs. Penny, and, to placate them, will permit their daughters to try to do more than they are capable of. Godden's stock characters of Lion and Mr. Felix appear—Lion simply a dance instructor, but Mr. Felix much more central. Chiding Madame for her shallowness, as he does in *A Candle for St. Jude,* Mr. Felix represents the voice of authentic art and is a fairy-godfather figure to Doone, recognizing his talent, encouraging him as a dancer, and teaching him to play the piano. When he dies early in the novel, Mr. Felix leaves his magnificent Steinway to the boy. Doone does not discover this gift until much later on, however, when he, a proficient dancer at twelve, is at the prestigious ballet academy Queen's Chase and has been earnestly wishing for a Steinway for a long time.

The contrast between the talented, fair, but shallow-minded Caroline and the more serious dancers Lollie and Hilda in *A Candle for St. Jude* is enlarged in *Thursday's Children* in the opposition between Crystal and Ruth Sherrin, the daughter of Madame Tamara's cleaning woman. Mrs. Sherrin, it turns out, was once a fine dancer herself, and her daughter's dedication and skill, which Doone recognizes and respects, irritate Crystal, causing her to declare Ruth an enemy. Crystal and Ruth soon go on to study at the ballet school of the famous dancer Ennis Glyn, where Crystal's shallowness continues to reveal itself. Ms. Glyn recognizes Doone's talent and, unbeknown to Doone's father, accepts him as a non-paying student. Doone thrives, no longer feeling like a "disregarded grub"; instead, it is as if the threads of a cocoon were breaking and he were being "forced out into the light" (87). When a jealous Crystal tells their father that Doone is studying dance, Pa attacks Ma as "ignorant of what your children are or should be" (95–96). To assuage his guilt for this attack, he permits Crystal to continue at Ms. Glyn's school but forbids Doone to do so.

The world of art has claimed Doone, however, and as one of a panel of dance experts will later say with religious fervor, there are children "born with a talent so strong that already it was dedicated as if it did not belong to the child but he to it; for what could be called an echo of the Gospel's 'Ye have not chosen me, but I have chosen you'" (128). Doone is "marked" for art, and Miss Glyn goes to Pa and persuades him to observe Doone secretly. When he does so, Pa undergoes a conversion experience equivalent to a religious one, now becoming completely devoted to his son's success as a dancer, defending him against his other sons' mockery and against Ma's preference for Crystal. Along with Crystal and Ruth, Doone applies to and is accepted at Queen's Chase, a beautiful, fairy-tale structure set in an Edenic park where deer roam. Thus, the world of art makes princes and princesses of even poor children, superseding class origins.

Despite their shared nobility in the world of dance, at Queen's Chase Crystal continues to treat Doone like Cinderfella, persuading him that he is a fairy changeling, that this is why Ma dislikes him, and that he was selected for a role as Oberon's page only because he has dark skin. Doone believes her and refuses to dance. When the ballet mistress coaxes the truth out of Doone, Crystal is chastised for bullying. While Doone is punished for his disobedience by not being allowed to dance in "The Dream," he learns the important lesson that a true artist never permits anything to interfere with his art.

More and more, Doone belongs to the world of dance. As Mrs. Challoner, head of Queen's Chase, observes, "these children come to belong to us more than to their parents" (163). Indeed, Doone yearns to remain at Queen's Chase for the Christmas holidays as Crystal tries to persuade him to sacrifice dance to save money for Pa, whose business is failing. But Doone, more sure of himself now, rejects Crystal's concept of nobility as sacrifice for the nobility of the world of dance.

Thursday's Children (as in the nursery rhyme, "Thursday's Child has far to go") is a fairy tale with a happy ending, in which the young protagonists, after many trials and with the help of donor figures both male and female, attain their full reward. Doone and Crystal will dance and be recognized for themselves, the utmost nobility. Crystal, despite her flaws, yearns for her better self, to live up to her name. "I wish I was pure," she cries, "all of one piece"; she blames Ma for being mixed up in her thinking and projecting unrealistic hopes onto her. Doone, she says, is not spoiled, "because you left him alone." This is a point often made in Godden's books for and about children; those fortunate children who somehow manage to avoid their parents' notice seem to thrive, finding their own resources, making their own "mark." It is orphaned, abandoned, or unpreferred children (Lovejoy, Ripsie, Emily, for example) who in the end most often achieve the nobility of their inner selves. Now Ma leaves Crystal to her own redemption, telling her, "At least . . . I believed in you. If you don't believe in yourself, that's not my fault" (166). Crystal still has trials by fire to endure before she can bring her component parts together, but in the end she will.

"Will" is here again, as always, an essential word in Godden's work. Doone longs for a Steinway, and when Mr. Felix's "will" is discovered, Doone has his wish fulfilled. But if Crystal also achieves her "will" to purify herself, it is only after she makes more trouble. She erases a music tape so that Doone, the only one who knows the music, will be asked to play the piano rather than dance at an important recital. But when Doone is accused of erasing the tape, Crystal defends him even at her own risk. She must also overcome her jealousy of Ruth, with whom she vies for a lead role in the attractive Yuri Koszorz's ballet.

Despite her flirtation with Yuri, in which she leads him on to kiss her as an adult, the role goes to Ruth, and Crystal considers suicide. At fifteen, she feels "too young and too old" and wishes she could be a child again (224). She runs away from Queen's Chase to her friend Val, who is largely unsupervised by her wealthy parents, and is tempted by the drugs Val steals from her doctor mother's cabinet. Following Val's advice, she decides, "If I want something, I go and get it" (229), and so goes to Yuri's house. But she sees him with another young dancer and runs away. Intending to take a train to her married brother Will's house (his name seems to emphasize her wish to purify her own "will"), she finds herself on a train headed back to school. Seeing this as fate, Crystal accepts the reality of her own limitations: "perhaps too, a new part of her had been born, a new resolve" (236), she thinks.

Arriving at Queen's Chase after dark, Crystal spends the night asleep in the park, awakening to see the dawn for the first time, a dawn like that in the Garden of Eden. Surrounded by deer and washed by dew, she is indeed closer to her true self than ever before. Colliding with Doone and Mrs. Challoner, Crystal learns that Ruth is sick with stage fright (she will ultimately become a choreographer, not a dancer) and that she has the part she yearned for. Mrs. Challoner orders Crystal to pull herself together (something she has been trying to do) and dance even though she no longer wishes to. Thus Crystal, like Doone, learns that art supersedes the individual. Now she is able to acknowledge that Doone is the master dancer in the family, although Ruth graciously assures Crystal that she is. But both Penny children dance triumphantly in the school production, Doone even being introduced to the queen. Mrs. Challoner's godlike words earlier in the book to Crystal, "Let Doone be Doone" and "Crystal be Crystal" (185), have been realized.

Fu-Dog

Fu-Dog provides a good transition to *Listen to the Nightingale,* Godden's third book with a balletic theme, which was published eight years after *Thursday's Children.* A dog will be at the center of *Listen to the Nightingale,* and it is the image of a dog, both worldly and otherworldly, about which *Fu-Dog*—a brightly colored children's picture book—revolves.

Resembling a dragon, the Fu-Dog was traditionally used to guard Chinese temples and palaces. The toy Fu-Dog, given to Li-la as a gift by her Chinese great-uncle, whom she and her brother, Malcolm, have never met, will, much as the dolls in Godden's doll stories, help the two children develop initiative, self-integration, and a sense of community.

Li-La and Malcolm are one-quarter Chinese, their mother being half Chinese and their father English. The two cultures do not entirely meld in their household. Li-la is so anglicized, for example, that she has to ask her mother what Chinese people eat. The Chinese in-laws see the children's father as too "rough and ready"[3]; their father, reciprocally, dislikes the Chinese part of the family and says he hates Chinese food.

If harmony is missing from the house of her own self, Li-La finds harmony in the gift sent by her great-uncle, a model of an intricately carved Chinese town with a mysterious blue-robed figure seated inside. In a quest for her roots, Li-La persuades Malcolm to join her on a trip to Chinatown. Like Hugh and Caddie in *The Battle of the Villa Fiorita* and Gregory and Janet in *The Kitchen Madonna,* the children set off alone, telling their parents they are going to visit their paternal grandmother. The story dismisses this lie with a rather cavalier, "Of course the children did not go to Granny" (chapter 2). But in Godden's fiction, as we have seen, as in fairy tales, parental aid and protection are often extraneous to the child's fundamental quest for selfhood; the child must somehow get on with his or her journey parentless in order to meet the requisite internal and external helpers. Since this is a children's book in which Fu-Dog, like the dolls in Godden's doll stories, may be seen to serve as an externalization of internal needs and ideal images, it is certain that those helpers will be encountered.

Fu-Dog helps the children enlarge their vision, telling Li-La to hold him up to her eye to see that he "can be as big as the sky, which I can fill." *Fu* means "me" in Chinese, and in enlarging her vision of the dog, Li-La expands her vision of her true self. Fu-Dog helps the children move both physically and emotionally, and when a train conductor asks, "Are you travelling alone?" Fu-Dog peeps out from Li-La's sleeve, inspiring Malcolm to reply, "We're travelling with Mr. Fu" (chapter 2), that is, we are on a journey with ourselves. When the first sight of London threatens to overwhelm them with doubts—"We shouldn't have come," says Malcolm—he seems to hear Fu reply, "We have come" (chapter 3). Fu even gives the children traffic directions; the taxi driver locates their great-uncle's restaurant by the two stone Fu-Dogs outside. Finally, the children astonish their younger uncle, who is amazed at their unescorted arrival, by telling him, "Fu-Dog brought us" (chapter 4).

At a festival parade, however, Li-La loses Fu-Dog and Malcolm is knocked down and badly hurt. The disheartened girl is comforted by Great Uncle, who, with his traditional blue robe and long beard, is very unlike her businesslike younger uncle. Great Uncle takes Li-La to the backyard of his London house, which has been scrupulously re-created as a Chinese garden, and tells her that Fu is a spirit dog and that the time has come for him to return to his ancestors. "Spirits come and go," he says. "But," asks Li-La, "do they go and come?" The answer to this question is, "In all sorts and sizes" (chapter 5). Great Uncle claps his hands, and a real dog, a golden Pekingese much resembling Fu-Dog, is brought to Li-La. To show that she understands the connection between the two dogs, Li-La names the Pekingese Fu-Dog II. Now she understands that everything Great Uncle touches turns to gold, and that all things in life are interrelated.

To demonstrate this truth further, Li-la's parents arrive, and, miraculously, they are not angry at their children's behavior. Li-La's father even professes, for the first time, to like Chinese food, saying, "I have to eat my words." Li-La is amazed that anyone can eat words: "There seemed no end to the strange things grown-ups could do" (chapter 6). Li-La's comment points not only to the gap that often exists between the adult's and the child's perceptions but also to the truth that for Godden, as the reader has seen in so much of this author's work, words hold the fruit of meaning; as in the Garden of Eden, to eat of the fruit of knowledge is to be transformed. The fruit/food/words Li-La's father eats are Chinese. In so doing, he helps Li-La and Malcolm integrate their rejected selves.

Now, though still depressed because he couldn't save Fu-Dog I, Malcolm begins to recover, and he hears Fu-Dog's voice assuring him that Malcolm's efforts to save him were heroic. Great Uncle gives Malcolm a bicycle to let him know it is all right to move forward with his life. The children and Great Uncle plan a Chinese ceremony to help send Fu-Dog I to his ancestors. Later, when Li-La returns home, she realizes that the secret garden of her uncle and his helping figure, Fu-Dog, can be accessed through the power of the imagination. The story ends on a note of fulfillment as the children learn that losses can be healed through the power of the internal eye/I, which can hold onto beloved images even when absent. This ability to retain lost or absent images from the past or present through imagination helps the children develop a sense of continuity and community that embraces all aspects of the self.

Great Grandfather's House

Although the child, Keiko, in *Great Grandfather's House* is Japanese rather than Chinese and is initially bad- rather than good-natured, in both *Great Grandfather's House* and *Fu-Dog* westernized little children learn to appreciate their cultural roots through the mediation of a benevolent elder. In both books, the image of the traditional home facilitates the integration of all aspects of the child's self.

Keiko's transformation is framed by the opening statement "I don't like Great Grandfather's house"[4] and the closing statement "I so like Great Grandfather's house." Keiko is a seven-year-old girl whose parents leave her at her great-grandparents' house in the Japanese countryside after suddenly announcing a three-month trip to England. As so many of Godden's books have demonstrated, such abandonment, while precipitous and initially painful, will open the child in unexpected ways. Not only will Keiko's rude and restless nature be tempered by the manners Old Mother and Great Grandfather will inculcate in her—manners that, as Keiko learns, prevent the wheels of life from grinding harshly—but she will learn to open herself to the sounds of the universe around her, to the "ssrh" of the bamboos, the "scritch" of Old Mother's hens, the "tsui bii" of Yoji's titmouse, and, ultimately, the fullness of her own nature.

Yoji is Keiko's six-year-old cousin, whose parents have also left him at Great Grandfather's house. A quiet, sensitive boy, he plays a bamboo flute and sails boats made of walnut shells he's made with Great Grandfather. Gradually, Keiko learns to share in Yoji's quiet games and fantasies. She comes to love Yoji's toad and joins Yoji in enacting a Japanese version of "The Princess and the Golden Ball," in which, dressed as a Japanese princess, Keiko agrees to kiss the toad to retrieve the golden ball (of selfhood). But Keiko's natural energies take over, and she squeezes Toad too hard, causing him to fall to the ground seemingly dead. Toad revives, but Yoji is furious, vowing Keiko will never hold anything of his again.

The two children reconcile, although Yoji keeps his vow. Keiko increasingly learns how to be still by enacting small Japanese rituals; watching Great Grandfather, a famous artist, paint the seasonal changes; and listening to the Japanese fairy tales that enrich the book itself. Yet circumstances seem to draw Keiko to disaster. Once, role-playing nature myths, Keiko and Yoji have a fierce argument when the boy refuses to let Keiko take the role of the "masculine" Wind God. As Keiko jumps up in fury at Yoji's chauvinism, the weather mirrors the children's anger and it rains fiercely; Keiko accidentally breaks Old Mother's precious bowls.

While Old Mother is not angry, she wishes for Keiko to become more gentle. Keiko finds the needed middle ground between female softness and strength in a scene in which, ironically, she tenderly holds Yoji's most precious possession—himself. Yoji, who is overly insistent on his

own masculine rightness, must also temper his spirit. Wearing her westernized rubber boots, having refused the more traditional straw ones,
Keiko comes across Yoji lying frozen, unconscious in the snow, and calls
for help while rubbing her cousin's hands and wrapping him in her coat.
Here Keiko has brought all aspects of herself—her western-style assert-
iveness and her new capacity for nurturing—to bear in saving Yoji. She
warms back to life not only Yoji's body but also his spiritual alter ego,
Titmouse, which lay frozen beside the boy.

Like *The River, Little Plum,* and many Godden books, *Great Grandfather's House* ends with a ritual celebration—here, aptly, New Year's Day,
with Keiko and Yoji in traditional dress. When the children's parents
arrive to take them home, Keiko is not ready to leave. Indeed, she is as
unrecognizable as the Grey children are at the end of *The Greengage
Summer.* "'Is this Keiko?' asked her Papa and Mamma: a little girl who . . .
moved gracefully with small steps in her purple kimono" (71–72). That
Keiko has not, however, lost her impulsive nature entirely, is demonstrated
as she grabs Yoji and pulls him headlong down the slippery steps.
Although the children must travel home in wet clothing, the author
relates that Great Grandfather gave Keiko a "twinkle and a pat" as he
shut the car door and that "Old Mother gave her encouraging nods" (75),
suggesting the elders' understanding that Keiko must retain aspects of her
impulsive self. Keiko is well on the way to building a house of self in which
she can live comfortably in rubber boots and blue kimono, in which
impulse and restraint dwell side by side.

Listen to the Nightingale

In *Listen to the Nightingale,* the third of Godden's ballet books, the focus
is, as in *Thursday's Children,* again on a child. In this case, it is Lottie, a
girl, who brings to mind Lollie of *A Candle for St. Jude.* The perspective
in this book, however, is more wholly that of the child than in Godden's
earlier books with a balletic setting: "She saw him and he saw her,"[5] the
story begins, citing the onset of a love affair between ten-year-old Lottie
and the Prince Charles Cavalier Spaniel that she saves from a boy who
has stolen him from a pet shop.

Lottie is on her way to be photographed for her audition at Queen's
Chase after years of studying at Madame Holbein's school. Like Madame
in *A Candle for St. Jude,* Madame Holbein[6] in *Listen to the Nightingale* is a
famous dancer; she is, again like her predecessor, in love with Lionel Ray
(Lion), who in this book is Hilda Frost's dance partner. Also like

Madame Holbein in *A Candle for St. Jude,* Madame of *Listen to the Nightingale* was, in her youth, Niura, whose grandmother had told her to "listen to the nightingale." But unlike the earlier Madame, this one remembers why: "I think she was trying to tell me that, though I was a dancer first and foremost, there were still other things in the world that I should need," like "cats and dogs, flowers, books, parties, wine, and people of course." Lottie longs for all these things, and wishes "she could hear a nightingale" (4).

Lottie is an orphan whose mother, Henrietta, had been a great dancer and died giving birth to Lottie. It is not clear whether Henrietta was married to Lottie's father, who in any case disappeared when Lottie was a baby. Lottie lives with her aunt, in straitened circumstances, attending ballet school in exchange for her aunt's services as Madame Holbein's wardrobe mistress. Where in *A Candle for St. Jude* the cabinet on the stairs held Madame's dancing relics, here it holds Henrietta's. Madame Holbein recognizes Lottie's inherited talents and supports her progress as a dancer because she has "the body, the will, the strength and the talent to dance" (6). But for Lottie, Prince, the dog she rescues and keeps, becomes her nightingale, giving balance and hope to her life, which is bleak aside from her dancing.

Hiding the dog from her aunt, who cannot afford to feed it, Lottie wears herself out running home to the basement to share her lunch with him, and her dancing suffers for it. Hilda Frost, the dance teacher who takes over the school when Madame dies (perhaps the grown-up Hilda of *A Candle for St. Jude*), discovers that the dog is her distraction. Hilda attacks Lottie for wasting energy and ruining her chance to be a dancer perfect within her scope. Yet Lottie recalls that Madame, on her deathbed, had called for her and, addressing her as Niura, warned her again to "listen to the nightingale" (39).

If Madame Holbein of *A Candle for St. Jude* is a stock figure, the Madame of *Listen to the Nightingale* is altogether more humanized. In the earlier book, Madame feels perpetually used and ignored; in *Listen to the Nightingale,* although Madame Holbein complains—telling Lottie, "What nuisances you children have always been to me. . . . Using me and knowing so much better than your elders" (39–40)—she is proud and loving: "Some nuisances are worth it, no?" And if Lottie is similar in name to Lollie of *A Candle for St. Jude,* she is a three-dimensional girl, her heart broken by the seemingly irreparable chasm between her love of dancing and of Prince. Relief comes when Lion reveals that Madame herself had a dog, Glinka. Lottie decides to go to day school to remain near

Prince, the only danger being that she might do too well at the audition for Queen's Chase and have to leave her beloved dog. But Lottie's talent cannot be suppressed; to her dismay, she is admitted to the prestigious school.

After much anguish, Lottie solves the problem of what to do with Prince while away at school. She leaves him on the doorstep of Violetta, nicknamed "Vivi," a motherless young Italian girl she had met while out walking Prince. Vivi is crippled and carried everywhere by her wealthy father's chauffeur (it will emerge later that Vivi's mother had injured her in infancy during a drunken rage). Vivi, who has lived a passive, pampered life, is miserable and can only scream at the caretakers who have control over her body, leading Lottie to think, "Children can't do anything against grownups" (30). Prince gives Vivi the motivation to live up to her nickname, "Life," and Lottie the music of the nightingale she requires to live a balanced life and to feel she has something of her own.

For Lottie still has her own sense of inadequacy to overcome. On the ride up to Queen's Chase, she feels like less than "a one-parent child" (69). But once at Queen's Chase, she and her aunt experience the same wonder at its palatial ambience as Crystal and Doone experienced in *Thursday's Children*. At Queen's Chase, all children can achieve a nobility comparable to that of the dukes and duchesses who lived there in earlier days. At the school, the reader encounters again Ennis Glyn and Mrs. Challoner, and a new character, Salvador, who is a pampered, tormented version of Doone. Dark-skinned, like a "fairy-changeling," he is mischievous and boastful. Only his natural talents have earned him a place at Queen's Chase. Salvador, along with Irene, another version of Crystal (she is fair-haired, superficial, and deceitful), will cause Lottie great suffering at Queen's Chase. Irene, whom Lottie had befriended at the audition, betrays Lottie by scorning her aunt and Madame Holbein on a visit to Lottie's home and by revealing the secret Lottie has shared with her about Prince's origin. Once Salvador learns this secret, he holds it over Lottie's head as a threat and forces her to do his bidding, to give him all her pocket money and food, and to join him on midnight picnics: "I like making people do what I want, especially girls. Especially you" (138), he tells her.

Salvador's is a form of negative wishing, which is particularly destructive: "I'll be the magician . . . you'll be the genie," he says, calling Lottie "the slave of the ring" (139). Salvador is the terror of the school as well, the instructors calling him "impervious." As one teacher comments, however, Salvador "feels more deeply than almost any of the boys. That's why he behaves as he does. He knows he's a misfit" (108). Salvador really likes Lottie very much and is trying to get her attention. When her dancing loses its "zing" as a result of her starvation and sleepless nights and she faints, Salvador confesses his wrongdoing to the school and returns her money to her, suggesting that she use it to pay the pet store for Prince.

It turns out that Salvador is Vivi's brother and that his bad behavior stems from anger at his mother, whom he had seen hurt Vivi. Their restaurateur father, Mr. Ruffino, is so grateful to Lottie for helping Vivi that he has been visiting Lottie's aunt, whom he will ultimately marry. He pays the extra money to buy Prince, who will now be part of a complete family. While Holbein's school closes down and an era is over, Lottie learns, as her aunt has told her, that "things have to come and go" (182). Salvador claims to love Lottie and, reminiscent of Lovejoy and Tip in *An Episode of Sparrows,* promises to marry her when they grow up. Although Lottie says, "children don't fall in love" (190), as so much of Godden's work demonstrates, where there is a will there is almost always a way. The book concludes with thundering success for both children when they dance in "The Birthday of the Infanta," in which Prince has an important role—as a Prince Charles Cavalier Spaniel. Lottie, accompanied by Salvador, dances the lead when Irene is expelled for failing grades. The two children (along with Prince) are, like Doone, introduced to the queen. When asked by a journalist what was the most important thing she learned at Madame Holbein's, Lottie replies, "To listen to the nightingale" (198).

Prince, the nightingale Lottie took time for, has changed her life, bringing the Ruffino family into it, helping to make "The Birthday of the Infanta" the success it was, and helping Lottie feel more herself. Godden has reversed Emily's loss, described in *Breakfast with the Nikolides,* and, fifty years later, permitted a child to find and keep her identity by keeping the dog she loves rather than by following the more difficult path of loneliness, loss, and redemption through racking, but ultimately strengthening, pain.

Other Works

If Rumer Godden's work featuring children seems to highlight an increasing sureness of self toward the end of the century, it is interesting to look at the peripheral image of the child in her adult fiction written during the same period: in *The Dark Horse* (1981) and *Coromandel, Sea*

Change (1990), for example, where the child appears as an image of hope. *The Dark Horse* is the story of how the combined efforts of some nuns, a jockey, and a racehorse named Dark Invader save a convent. The fairy-tale tone of the story echoes that of the children's books of the period, and the story ends happily with a birth. A foal is bred by Dark Invader out of the mare Fairy-tale and is named Dark Legend, pointing to the theme of continuity and legend making that runs through many of Godden's stories of the 1980s.

Coromandel, Sea Change also ends with the birth of a child whose life holds more hope than that of the book's protagonists. Mary Browne and her tyrannical diplomat husband, Blaise, are staying at Patna Hall, a hotel on the Coromandel Coast in India. They argue over Mary's involvement in Indian politics and her friendship with Krishnan, the local candidate. That Mary is at heart an abandoned child is suggested by the fact that her diplomat father can never be located and by Blaise's physical as well as emotional abuse of her. Despite Blaise's claim that Mary is not a child but a married woman, Mary refuses to define herself that way, and after each visit with Krishnan feels more playful, free, and childlike. Indeed, if Krishnan is the image of the ideal mother, so is his feminine counterpart, Auntie Sanni, who owns Patna Hall and adopts Mary as a child of the house.

After one particularly fierce argument with Mary, Blaise impregnates their Indian servant and commits suicide by swimming in dangerous ocean waters. He is killed by a baby shark Mary had warned him about, perhaps symbolizing how harmful to the self and others denial of the childlike aspects of the self can be. With Blaise gone, Mary remains in India to do charity work and begin a new life. The newborn child of two continents is sent to live in England with his paternal grandparents, perhaps to emerge a new and better "blaze" of humanity.

The author's most recently published adult novel, *Pippa Passes* (1994), is yet another book with a balletic theme. *Pippa Passes* is set in Venice, where seventeen-year-old Pippa, the youngest member of the dance troupe, is the victim of an attempted seduction by the troupe's female chaperone. She rejects the chaperone ("passing" on the experience), protesting when the older woman refers to her as "little." Pippa's childlike name and her disregard of warnings about the chaperone, however, attest to her childlike nature. In this book, a mother figure fails to protect her charge, and it is unclear whether the "child" has developed adequate self-protective resources. The book concludes in some confusion, with Pippa unconvincingly asserting the importance of her career above all else while lamenting her rejection by the young gondolier she has pursued as intensely as the chaperone has pursued her.

It is difficult to know what to make of this book; of the choices it offers; of its picture of female sexual aggressiveness only hinted at in earlier books such as *Gypsy, Gypsy,* in autobiographical fragments, and in descriptions of the cloistered life. But that Rumer Godden retains the ability to surprise her readers with images of fulfilled and unfulfilled longing and hope is eminently clear.

Chapter Eight
Conclusion: The Child Itself

The question whether in Godden's vision of childhood children must be sacrificed on the altar of adult needs must be answered, in part, "yes." In her fiction for both adults and children, children often view themselves as helpless in the world of adults, as are the dog Don in *Breakfast with the Nikolides* and the Christlike donkey, Slippers, who is beaten by Blaise in *Coromandel, Sea Change.*

While children are sometimes merely, if painfully, overlooked or underestimated by busy or superficial parents—Gregory in *The Kitchen Madonna,* Doone in *Thursday's Children,* and Bonnie in *Mouse House,* for example—they are more often portrayed as orphans. Henrietta in *Gypsy, Gypsy,* Ivy in *The Story of Holly and Ivy,* Ripsie in *China Court,* and Kizzy in *The Diddakoi* fall into the first category. Lovejoy in *An Episode of Sparrows,* Tracy in *China Court,* Hugh and Caddie in *The Battle of the Villa Fiorita,* the Grey siblings in *The Greengage Summer,* and the young dragon of Og in the children's book of that name are among those who belong in the second category—those who have been physically abandoned by their parents. Yet another category of children includes those who suffer potentially life-threatening emotional and/or spiritual neglect at the hands of a parent or caretaker—as do Teresa and Moo in *Kingfishers Catch Fire,* Keith in *In This House of Brede,* and Apple in *The Dolls' House.*

Childhood is often portrayed as a brief interlude, invaded by early glimpses of betrayal and mortality. In *Breakfast with the Nikolides,* Louise's conflict with her husband engulfs Emily and leads Louise to lie to her daughter about Don's death; in *Kingfishers Catch Fire,* Teresa must cope with Sophie's inability to distinguish between her idealized view of childhood and reality and with her mother's deafness to her daughter's true needs; in *The River,* Harriet must learn to absorb her own guilt at her brother's death. In *An Episode of Sparrows,* the waif Lovejoy sees herself as a pinprick in the vortex of the universe; in *The Greengage Summer,* four children on their own as outsiders in a French village must struggle with the difficult question of defining the borderlines between good and evil, childhood and adulthood. The children learn that the boundary between childhood and adulthood is invisible, and if it is possible to be both good and evil, it is harder to move back and forth between the lands of childhood and adulthood once the boundary has been traversed.

In these books, in which children serve as protagonists, children feel "stretched" as they experience growing pains. Except for Sophie, adults are, on the whole, minor figures, frustrated in their ambitions. A sense emerges that although adults may reach out to fulfill wants, as a whole, circumstances will force them back home. How do children react to this pessimistic reality? Some, like Bogey, imitate Wordsworth's boy in "The Prelude," and die young. Bogey has no "wants" and seems to prefer the eternal childhood of death. Others, however, who want and will deeply, are driven to survive, and a nearly evolutionary sense that the next generation will do better seems to underlie the texts.

The sense of an interconnection between the lives of the young and the old, the living and the dead, pervades *Take Three Tenses* and *China Court*. The latter book has a fairy-tale quality of continuity between the generations who have lived at China Court over the past century. The happiness of the new generation in some way completes or absolves earlier, less fulfilled lives. Paradoxically, too, the outsider—in this case, the house's current owner, Mrs. Quin, who was once the orphan Ripsie, living on charity at China Court—has a better chance for happiness than the children raised in the confines of the traditional home.

For while a rooted home (something Godden herself never had) is desirable, it can also be stifling. As with Sophie in *Kingfishers Catch Fire*, it is tempting to follow one's star wherever it may lead. The children who grew up at China Court are not very happy. The child who is neglected or simply ignored is also free from the overprotection and overstructuring that can blur one's deepest wishes. The orphan figure, like Ripsie or Lovejoy, has already experienced the "vortex," has seen life from less delineated perspectives, and can thus inherit and live within tradition creatively.

And so, the other part of the answer to the question whether children must be sacrificed so that adults can fulfill their own needs is "not necessarily" or "perhaps, not finally." Godden seems to have a strong conviction that the universe and the child's imagination and willpower can indeed provide the wherewithal, the resources, for more than mere survival; they can provide for the integration of a strong self. Children have the ability to make use of integrating symbols, such as house, garden, river, temple (as do Ripsie, Lovejoy, Harriet, Nona, and Belinda); to project thoughts and emotions onto external, manageable images such as animals and dolls (again, Nona and Belinda, Sian, Mary, Emily, and

Charlotte); and to find helping figures in their peers, even when the relationship doesn't always run smoothly (Lovejoy/Tip, Nona/Tom, Gem/
Belinda, Selina/Tim, Lottie/Salvador).

As in fairy tales, the "motherless" child who "wants"—in both senses
of the word—can overcome obstacles by determined imagining and willing and may choose or be chosen by a literal or symbolic mother (or in
some cases, father) figure able to provide what is lacking. Examples of literal child/surrogate parent pairs include Lovejoy/Olivia Chesney, Ivy/Mrs.
Jones (and Holly/Ivy), Gregory/Marta, Kizzy/Olivia Brooke, Tibby/Miss
Pomeroy, Tracy/Mrs.Quin (formerly Ripsie), the young dragon/Matilda,
Doone/Beppo and Doone/Miss Glyn, Li-La/Great Uncle, Keiko/Great
Grandfather, Mary Browne/Krishnan, and Mary Browne/Auntie Sanni.

Examples of more symbolic "mother" figures include institutions like
the church (largely in books not focused on the child protagonist) and
vocations like art. Writing, ballet, painting—these represent worlds in
which, as the panel of dance experts comment in *Thursday's Children,*
there are children "born with a talent so strong that already it was dedicated as if it did not belong to the child but he to it" (128). The world of
art makes princes and princesses of children marked by it, eliminating
the marks of class connected to natural birth. Doone, Lollie, Lottie,
Gregory, Emily, Harriet—all are sustained by the nurturing umbilical
cord which connects them to their crafts.

Godden's work offers no one-sided answers but continues through
"truthful writing" to explore the possibilities for the integration of the
self. Although many of Godden's books may be read by young people or
adults, Godden's novels addressed to adult audiences on the whole
require more attention to the ambiguities of all answers, all conclusions.
The bleak ending of *The Battle of the Villa Fiorita,* for example, is coun-
teracted in part only by the reader's awareness of what the children have
learned about the complexities of life and love during their Italian
sojourn. There are no mitigating symbols here, only the thorns that
hedge Fanny in as she returns home. But the children have been
"stretched," and will, perhaps, if the experience has not shattered them,
be able in their own lives to find a compromise between home and chaos.

Commenting on the hopeful conclusion of *An Episode of Sparrows*
(written for adults), where the deus ex machina of Olivia's will saves
Lovejoy from the charity school, Godden observes that Lovejoy should
have "gone to school and been left there" for the successful artistic
denouement of her character and the book as a whole (Wintle and
Fisher, 292). In her children's books Godden offers less ambivalent, well-

earned images of hope. Her children's stories seem to follow a maxim suggested by Uri Shulevitz, a contemporary author and illustrator of children's books, in an anecdote that emphasizes the importance of maintaining a spirit of hope in children. Shulevitz asked students in his class in children's book illustration to picture a story in which twelve little fish swim into a cave-like structure that snaps shut each time a little fish enters it. The story is told from the perspective of the twelfth little fish. If that fish is also swallowed and cannot escape, Shulevitz suggests, the story is not for children because it does nothing to foster hope.[1]

Godden comments somewhat along the same lines: "I don't think it's done to write books for children where—this may sound awfully prissy—where evil triumphs. . . . And I suppose unconsciously, we want children to believe that good is stronger than evil" (Wintle and Fisher, 291). Children want Candy Floss to return to Jack, as they want Cinderella to marry the prince, Godden adds. Yet Godden's vision remains complex, for she also advocates no limits or simplified language in books for children and no categorizing of novels for young adults.[2]

As noted earlier, "truthful writing" for Godden requires the child to wrest his or her own selfhood out of the apparent chaos created by adults. From this perspective, Godden can be seen as one of the line of "modern fantasists" Sheila Egoff defines in *Thursday's Child,* a group that includes Lucy Boston, Philippa Pearce, and Penelope Lively. In these books of "enchanted realism," children's parents don't "play an active role in the events,"[3] and children struggle, on their own or with a surrogate parent-helper, toward maturity. Time is often seen as "multi-dimensional," as a "river," and childhood as a "continuum" (104). Much of "enchanted realism takes its aura from a house or from a narrow space," such as "a garden." In "these new fantasies the inner landscape of the mind is explored much more deeply and sensitively" than in earlier fantasies (105).

Egoff does not refer to Godden's books as examples of "enchanted realism," perhaps because stories like *Take Three Tenses* and *China Court* were not written for children. Nevertheless, like Philippa Pearce's *Tom's Midnight Garden* and Lucy Boston's *The Children of Green Knowe, Take Three Tenses* and *China Court* bring the extraordinary into the realm of the ordinary rather than the reverse, an aspect of Egoff's definition of "enchanted realism." And in these two Godden novels, as in children's books Egoff describes, "modern fantasy does not fit the two worlds back together" but "establishes fantasy as an 'edge' literature" (87). As characters move imperceptibly between worlds and/or time frames, the reader thinks not only of the invisible children in Boston's book and of the

child Hattie in Pearce's book but of the unseen children of *China Court*
and *Take Three Tenses,* who keep intruding on the present.

In some of Godden's books, as in Boston's and Pearce's, the bridges
"between the worlds of reality and fantasy no longer are seen as necessary"; transitions may take place as one hears a voice, turns one's back to
someone, or touches an object. Modern fantasists, as Egoff remarks in
Thursday's Child, "are likely to employ highly sophisticated techniques,
often derived from cinematography: three-dimensional viewing; slow
motion; fade-ins; superimposition; sharp, staccato dialogue; and fast-
pace cutting from scene to scene" (87).

Again, Egoff does not refer to Godden in the context of cinemato-
graphic writers. Many of Godden's techniques, however, seem to place her
in the company of the writers Egoff describes, as does the ease with which
several of her books have been translated into films. One thinks of
Godden's unorthodox use of tenses—referring to the past as the present
and vice versa and superimposing voices and images from each time frame
(as in *Take Three Tenses* and *China Court*); her use of dialogue between internal voices (as in *The River*); her unusual syntactical structures (described
below); and her use of multiple perspectives (as in *An Episode of Sparrows,*
where Olivia watches Lovejoy from her window, Lovejoy looks up at the
church window, and the priest looks down at Lovejoy in the garden).

It is perhaps no accident that the modern fantasists Egoff describes
are all women. While male writers such as Laurence Sterne and James
Joyce have experimented with the boundaries of traditional sentence and
paragraph structure, as recent linguistic explorations by feminist critics
demonstrate, the compulsion toward a syntactical experimentation that
breaks through the bounds of language and time is endemic to the contemporary woman writer's quest for her true voice.

In *A Room of One's Own,* Virginia Woolf highlighted the need for the
woman writer to free herself from the "sentence-as-definitive-judgment"
and to create one that could, as Sandra Gilbert and Susan Gubar state it
in *No Man's Land,* instead "sentence her to freedom,"[4] to create what
these authors refer to as a "vulvalogocentric" language to replace a patri-
archal, "phallogocentric" language, which focuses on defining, analyzing,
and labeling (270). Godden's own passionate engagement with language, her efforts to name or rename objects in her universe, to discover
their multiple and thereby true meanings, seems intuitively in line with
this compulsion toward definition of a new way of using words.

Gilbert and Gubar quote feminist critics such as Luce Irigary and
Hélène Cixous who ask readers to "imagine a female language which is

always in the process of weaving itself, of embracing itself with words, but also of getting rid of words in order not to become fixed, congealed in them" (230). Godden weaves together not only tenses but also contradictory movements and thoughts, often linking them with the conjunction, "but" rather than "and." Thus, conflict, which is so central to Godden's work, is not easily resolved by the sentence (in the linguistic sense or as orthodox judgment). Instead of the concept of "sentence-as-definitive-judgment," which so troubled Woolf, Godden's syntax sentences women (and men and children as well) to search for freedom as multiple perspectives and truths are woven together through time and language.

Let us consider, for example, the moment in *The Battle of the Villa Fiorita* when Fanny thinks about how passion for Rob has swept her up: "'If it was not meant to happen, why did God let it?' asked Fanny like a little girl. It was absurd to bring God into it, but, 'we were avoiding one another'"(92). Here, "but" shows the contradiction between Fanny's perception of herself as a child who bears no responsibility for her actions and the woman who, though conscious of the possible results of her attraction to forbidden fruit, wants to plead guiltlessness because she had tried to avoid Rob. The commas framing the "but" seem to highlight the weakness of the conjunction and underline the ambiguity of Fanny's situation.

The "but" appears more forceful in the voice of Fanny's twelve-year-old daughter Caddie when the arrival of Rob's daughter, Pia, is discussed: "'I want her to come,' said Fanny. 'When you love someone, you want to love the people they love.' 'But will you be able to?' asked Caddie" (193). In *The Peacock Spring,* Ravi, the Indian youth, in hiding from the authorities, is sowing seeds. He states his belief that some are doomed to wither: "'If they must, they must.' 'But you must sow them as carefully as you can,' said Hemanjo Sharma, who was his best—perhaps now his only friend."

"Hem was always anxious. 'Should you not,' he had asked, 'change your name?' But Ravi had only laughed. 'I am Ravi Bhattacharyo, good or bad'" (8). Here, the repeated use of the conjunction "but" early on in the book serves as a warning about a contradiction in Ravi's character: he is like the peacock, "so busy admiring his own train" that he forgets he has feet (frontispiece).

While the examples can be multiplied, one from Godden's third autobiography, *A House with Four Rooms,* will suffice to illustrate the impact of this disjunctive conjunction. On the ship to England following the crisis described at the end of *Kingfishers Catch Fire,* the ship's doctor asks Rumer, "'are you the family they tried to poison?' 'It wasn't poison, only drugs,' which was not quite true—Olwen had been given belladonna but I was trying not to make it too sensational—I still could not believe it myself but, 'it was only marijuana and ground glass,' I said. 'You might have died,' the doctor said" (21). In this instance, the first "but" is protective of the private self; the second, followed rather than preceded by the comma-pause, highlights a contradiction between the seriousness of the event and Godden's attempt to minimize it in an almost humorous but certainly shocking statement—as the ship's doctor easily perceives.

In her review of Godden's second autobiography, Janette Hospital sees Godden as "more a first-rate story-teller than a major literary figure" and offers *A Time to Dance, No Time to Weep,* as an example of stylistic weakness. Godden's autobiographical style is "best characterized as pell-mell and more than a little artless. It is as though we are getting breathless anecdotes on the run." We are mesmerized but aware of "frequently clumsy locutions, of a number of grammatical blunders, of sloppy syntax, of a punctuation style that can only be called quixotic."[5] But the very stylistic quirks Hospital points to in fact make Godden an important literary figure, for in place of the concept of "sentence-as-definitive-judgment," which so troubled Virginia Woolf, Godden's syntax reflects her characters' inner struggles for truth in a fashion that is most artful indeed.

Thus, in *A Time to Dance, No Time to Weep,* Godden describes her resentment of an early boyfriend's attempts to control her: "I rode, raced, went out under his protection and I did not want to be protected, I wanted adventure. Perhaps it is Mam's Quaker upbringing, passed in a way to us, that makes me seldom want possessions; now I felt as if I were weighed down with them. I wanted to live light and free—I have always wanted that" (58).

Far from quixotic, Godden's punctuation reflects her recalled inner landscape—the run-on re-creating her frenzied desire for adventure; the semicolon, with its formal stop, echoing the meaning of the clause that bows her down; and the dash commenting on the timelessness of her quest for freedom.

The syntax by which children discover themselves is an extension of that through which Godden's women free themselves. Godden writes of a twelve-year-old girl who "appears two or three times in books of mine" and by whom "I was haunted" (Wintle and Fisher, 290–92). Indeed, Godden was haunted to the degree that she would attempt to write a childless book, *In This House of Brede,* to avoid her spectral image. These girls, like Wordsworth's boy of Winander in "The Prelude," stand at the bridge between childhood and maturity. The question whether and how they will survive the transition from innocence to experience is central to their haunting quality, and indeed the internal language by which they struggle toward growth echoes the dreamlike quality of this in-between space.

One of these girls is Caddie of *The Battle of the Villa Fiorita.* At the end of the book, when Caddie is distressed because Hugh and Pia have disappeared together and it seems as if Rob will finally take Fanny away, "it came to her that she had lost everything now: lost Topaz, lost Hugh, lost the battle; in a few minutes, she would lose Fanny; everyone, everything she really cared for; she was Caddie alone, with nothing and no one to hold onto. She would always be alone now and it was then that Caddie made a startling discovery: she was alone, defeated, she had lost everything—and she was still herself, Caddie, still all right. Then it doesn't matter what happens to you, thought Caddie. You go on" (281). In this passage, semicolons delineate the separate units of Caddie's flow of consciousness; they mark her dawning realization of self—until the dash signals the flash of understanding by which she perceives the continuity of selfhood.

Harriet, in *The River,* a thoughtful, creative girl who feels herself to be something of a misfit, is the second example of the child who haunted Godden. The inner landscape of her thoughts is also expressed in a flow of creative movements forward and backward that plays with traditional sentence structure:

> Harriet sighed. Latin, and algebra, and music and other things: eating liver, having an injection, seeing a mad pai-dog—how did Bea manage to take them all so quietly? How? She could not, nowadays, aspire to Bea. . . . and her mind went off on a rapid Harriet canter of its own, too rapid for stops. Will-I-get-hookworm-you-get-all-kinds-of-worms-in-India-and-diseases-too-there-is-a-leper-in-the-bazaar-no-nose-and-his-fingers-dropping-off-him-if-I-had-no-fingers-I-couldn't-learn-music-could-I-no-March-of-the-Men-of-Harlech. (5–6)

The third adolescent by whom Godden was haunted is Cecil in *The Greengage Summer.* The language of this book, written in the past tense, does not reflect the immediacy of *The Battle of the Villa Fiorita* or *The River,* but it does reflect Cecil's attempt to understand her experience through language. When she surprises Eliot in a decadent mood, she is

startled by the sight of an unknown man: "This was another Eliot than
the kind Englishman of last night; someone cold and . . . ruthless, I
thought. That was a strange word to come into my head when I did not
know the meaning of 'ruth.' 'Eliot's eyes are not blue,' Hester was to
say. 'They are green-grey, like pebbles.' Now, close to him on the stairs,
I saw they were grey and coldly angry. 'What are you doing down
here?'" (38)

While it is the woman or girl whose consciousness is most often center stage in Godden's books, sentence structure also reflects the inner life
of the young male protagonist in *The Kitchen Madonna*. Like Harriet,
Gregory is perceived as—and perceives himself as—a misfit. He is an
artist at heart, but, unlike Harriet's brother, he is a survivor—through
art. As Gregory creates the Kitchen Madonna out of scraps, the sentence
structure follows the steady creative flow of his mind; his idea evolves
slowly as the sentence unfolds. (Is this in contrast to the pell-mell quality of Harriet's female creativity?) Semicolons set off modifications of the
creative process, and the dashes signal his excitement as the solution
approaches despite difficulties:

> For the flower that gave the picture its name, "Our Lady of the Unfading
> Flower," he did not choose one of Madame Ginette's flowers; they looked
> wrong, too heavy and pale; he tried a Japanese water flower, drying it
> carefully when it had opened out, but laid on the picture it seemed to
> stand out too much. In the end, his tongue held anxiously in his teeth,
> Gregory copied it—"I can't really paint, you know"—but its shape and
> the faint-pink of water flowers seemed right and, "It doesn't look too
> grown up for us or for Marta," said Janet. Then, "What will you use for
> the border?" she asked. (75)

Godden's unusual use of the punctuation "and," rather than ", and"
toward the end of this quotation suggests that the conjunction serves not
merely to link the two clauses but to introduce and highlight Janet's
important response to the newly created object d'art. As she becomes
increasingly swept up in Gregory's creativity, Janet's thoughts mingle
with his: "Then" signals the children's shared search for a solution, the
capital letter suggesting Janet's new input, the run-on linking them
both in one creative process, much as in *Listen to the Nightingale* a run-on
links Lottie and the dog Prince in their love-at-first-sight encounter:
"She looked at him, he looked at her, and it was as if an invisible thread
stretched across the street and tied them together, tight" (1).

Writing of her beloved Hans Christian Andersen, Godden relates an anecdote in which a "pedantic young gentleman began to pick an Andersen poem to pieces; he found flaw after flaw in line after line," until finally, the hostess's "small daughter spoke. 'Look,' she said, pointing to the poem, 'There is one little word you haven't scolded yet.' The one little word was 'and.'"[6]

It may be said that Godden herself has "scolded" every one of her own words, so carefully chosen are they to reflect meaning. As Godden commented in her "Opening Speech for the Children's Books of the Year Exhibition" in 1976: "It takes courage to tell a story, to endure the discipline of writing it, and doing that for children is a far more difficult art than writing a novel: courage not to listen to what people tell you, to what your publishers say will sell. Even they do not always know."[7]

"Which 'she' is she?" asks Elaine Moss, putting the question Rumer Godden poses to the multifaceted goddess Shiva (in *Shiva's Pigeons*) to the author herself. Godden's answer, like Shiva's, is "All": "disorderly woman," "brilliantly successful author for adults," "loved children's storyteller," "the mother and grandmother who knows she must allow her writing to be interrupted by social claims," "the dedicated artist and researcher whose work is her life," and more. In Godden's oeuvre, as with Shiva, symbol of India, "Pairs of opposites . . . do not clash, but rather give her a peculiar richness."[8]

Godden's ability to make her readers more familiar with all four rooms of the house of the self has indeed made her a woman for all seasons. As Orville Prescott writes of her:

A few writers can persuade their readers that they have cast a ray of light into the secret places of the heart, that they have increased by a mite the sum of human understanding about life and love and death, grief and loneliness and the misery of growing up. Theirs is no mean feat. It is a high art to distil the essence of experience into fiction. And to do so without adding to the general din, in a quiet voice, with taste, simplicity and sure technical craftsmanship, is to contribute something rare and fine to a world sadly in need of it.[9]

Notes and References

Preface

    1. Rumer Godden, "The Will to Write," *Writer,* May 1985, 13; hereafter cited in text.

    2. Rumer Godden, *A House with Four Rooms* (London: Macmillan, 1989); hereafter cited in text.

    3. W. Y. Tindall, "Rumer Godden, Public Symbolist," *English Journal* 41 (March 1952): 117; hereafter cited in text.

    4. Hassell Simpson, *Rumer Godden* (New York: Twayne, 1973), 44; hereafter cited in text.

Chapter One

    1. Rumer Godden, *A Time to Dance, No Time to Weep* (New York: William Morrow, 1987), 218; hereafter cited in text.

    2. Rumer and Jon Godden, *Two under the Indian Sun* (New York: Alfred A. Knopf, 1966), vii; hereafter cited in text.

    3. Thomas Dukes, "Evoking the Significance: The Autobiographies of Rumer Godden," *Women's Studies* 20 (1991): 16; hereafter cited in text.

    4. See Rumer Godden's essay, "Shining Popocatepetl: Poetry for Children," in *Horn Book Magazine* 64 (May 1988): 304–5, for the author's insights into the importance of poetry in a child's life.

Chapter Two

    1. Rumer Godden, *Breakfast with the Nikolides* (New York: Viking Press, 1964), 18; hereafter cited in text.

    2. Rumer Godden, *Take Three Tenses: A Fugue in Time* (Boston: Little, Brown, 1945), 147; hereafter cited in text.

    3. Rumer Godden, *The River* (Boston: Little, Brown, 1946), 5; hereafter cited in text.

    4. Margaret and Michael Rustin, *Narratives of Love and Loss: Studies in Modern Children's Fiction* (London/New York: Verso, 1987), 85; hereafter cited in text.

    5. Rumer Godden, *The Dolls' House* (New York: Viking Press, 1948), 12; hereafter cited in text.

    6. Rumer Godden, "The Writer Must Become as a Child," *Writer,* July 1955, 229; hereafter cited in text.

7. Justin Wintle and Emma Fisher, *The Pied Pipers: Interviews with the Influential Creators of Children's Literature* (London: Paddington Press, 1973), 293; hereafter cited in text.

8. Rumer Godden, *A Candle for St. Jude* (New York: Viking Press, 1948), 86; hereafter cited in text.

9. Rumer Godden, *Chinese Puzzle* (London: Peter Davies, 1936), 3; hereafter cited in text.

10. Godden, Rumer, *Gypsy, Gypsy* (Boston: Little, Brown, 1940), 12; hereafter cited in text.

Chapter Three

1. Rumer Godden, *The Mousewife* (New York: Viking Press, 1951), 9; hereafter cited in text.

2. Rumer Godden, *Mouse House* (New York: Viking Press, 1957), 36–37; hereafter cited in text.

3. Rumer Godden, *Kingfishers Catch Fire* (New York: Viking Press, 1953), 3; hereafter cited in text.

4. Rumer Godden, "On Words," *Writer,* September 1962, 17; hereafter cited in text.

5. Eleanor Cameron, *The Green and Burning Tree: On the Writing and Enjoyment of Children's Books* (Boston: Little, Brown, 1962), 287.

6. Rumer Godden, *An Episode of Sparrows* (New York: Viking Press, 1955), 9; hereafter cited in text.

7. Rumer Godden, *The Greengage Summer* (New York: Viking Press, 1958), 17; hereafter cited in text.

Chapter Four

1. Frank Eyre, *British Children's Books of the Twentieth Century* (New York: Dutton, 1973), 68; hereafter cited in text.

2. Lois Kuznets, *When Toys Come Alive: Narratives of Animation, Metamorphosis, and Development* (New Haven: Yale University Press, 1994), 111; hereafter cited in text.

3. Rumer Godden, *Four Dolls: Impunity Jane, The Fairy Doll, The Story of Holly and Ivy, and Candy Floss,* (New York: Greenwillow Books, 1983), 93; hereafter cited in text.

4. Rumer Godden, *Miss Happiness and Miss Flower* (New York: Viking Press, 1961), 1; hereafter cited in text.

5. Rumer Godden, *Little Plum* (New York: Viking Press, 1963), 50; hereafter cited in text.

6. Rumer Godden, *Home Is the Sailor* (New York: Viking Press, 1964), 3; hereafter cited in text.

Chapter Five

1. Rumer Godden, *China Court: The Hours of a Country House* (New York: Viking Press, 1961), 64; hereafter cited in text.
2. Bruno Bettelheim, *The Uses of Enchantment: The Meaning and Importance of Fairy Tales* (New York: Vintage Books, 1977), 286; hereafter cited in text.
3. Rumer Godden, *The Battle of the Villa Fiorita* (New York: Viking Press, 1963), 128–29; hereafter cited in text.
4. Rumer Godden, *The Kitchen Madonna* (New York: Viking Press, 1967), 9; hereafter cited in text.
5. Rumer Godden, *In This House of Brede* (New York: Viking Press, 1969), 267; hereafter cited in text.
6. Rumer Godden, *Gone: A Thread of Stories* (New York: Viking Press, 1968), vii; hereafter cited in text.

Chapter Six

1. Rumer Godden, *The Old Woman Who Lived in a Vinegar Bottle* (New York: Viking Press, 1972), preface; hereafter cited in text.
2. Rumer Godden, *The Diddakoi* (New York: Puffin, 1975), 70; hereafter cited in text.
3. Rumer Godden, *Mr. McFadden's Hallowe'en* (New York: Viking Press, 1975), 107; hereafter cited in text.
4. Rumer Godden, *The Peacock Spring* (New York: Viking Press, 1975), 93; hereafter cited in text.
5. Rumer Godden, *The Rocking Horse Secret* (New York: Viking Press, 1978), 31; hereafter cited in text.
6. Rumer Godden, *A Kindle of Kittens* (New York: Viking Press, 1979), unpaginated; hereafter cited in text.

Chapter Seven

1. Rumer Godden, *The Dragon of Og* (New York: Viking Press, 1981), 1; hereafter cited in text.
2. Rumer Godden, *Thursday's Children* (New York: Dell, 1984), 6; hereafter cited in text.
3. Rumer Godden, *Fu-Dog* (New York: Viking Press, 1990), chapter 2, unpaginated; hereafter cited in text.
4. Rumer Godden, *Great Grandfather's House* (New York: Greenwillow Books, 1993), 5, 75; hereafter cited in text.
5. Rumer Godden, *Listen to the Nightingale* (New York: Viking Press, 1992), 1; hereafter cited in text.

6. Madame Holbein is a recurrent figure in Godden's work, and the author has referred to her as a "stock figure." See letter to Hassell Simpson, 30 August 1963, cited in his *Rumer Godden,* 52.

Chapter Eight

1. Uri Shulevitz is the author and illustrator of numerous children's books, including *Dawn* (New York: Farrar, Straus and Giroux, 1984). The observation was made in a class held at The New School in New York City in the late 1970s or early 1980s.

2. Wintle and Fisher, *The Pied Pipers,* 293, quote Godden: "a novel that is simplified for children will always fail"; see also Godden's devastating spoof of a letter from Beatrix Potter's publisher requesting that she write in monosyllables, first published as "An Imaginary Correspondence" in *Horn Book Magazine* 38 (August 1963) 197–206; reprinted in Virginia Haviland's *Children and Literature: Views and Reviews* (Glenview, Ill.: Scott, Foresman and Co., 1973), 133–39.

3. Sheila Egoff, *Thursday's Child: Trends and Patterns in Contemporary Children's Literature* (Chicago: American Library Association, 1987), 97; hereafter cited in text.

4. Sandra Gilbert and Susan Gubar, *No Man's Land: The Place of the Woman Writer in the Twentieth Century,* vol. 1, *The War of the Words* (New Haven: Yale University Press, 1988), 230; hereafter cited in text.

5. Janette Turner Hospital, "Adventure Was What She Got," *New York Times Book Review,* 3 January 1988, 13.

6. Rumer Godden, "Hans Andersen, Writer," *Horn Book Magazine* 66 (September 1990): 557.

7. Rumer Godden, "Opening Speech for Children's Books of the Year Exhibition," *Signal Magazine* 21 (September 1976): 117.

8. Elaine Moss, "Rumer Godden: Prince of Storytellers," *Signal Magazine* 17 (May 1975): 60.

9. Orville Prescott, *In My Opinion: An Inquiry into the Contemporary Novel* (Indianapolis: Bobbs-Merrill, 1952), 287.

Selected Bibliography

PRIMARY WORKS

Books for Children and Young Adults

Candy Floss. New York: Viking Press, 1960. London: Macmillan, 1960.

The Diddakoi. New York: Viking Press, 1972. London: Macmillan, 1973. New York: Puffin Books, 1975.

The Dolls' House. Illustrated by Dana Saintsbury. London: Michael Joseph, 1947. New York: Viking Press, 1948.

The Dragon of Og. Illustrated by Pauline Baynes. New York: Viking Press, 1981.

The Fairy Doll. New York: Viking Press, 1956. London: Macmillan, 1956.

Four Dolls. New York: Greenwillow Books, 1983. London: Macmillan, 1983. Includes *Candy Floss, Impunity Jane, The Fairy Doll,* and *The Story of Holly and Ivy.*

Fu-Dog. London: Julia MacRae Books, 1989. Illustrated by Valerie Littlewood. New York: Viking Press, 1990.

Great Grandfather's House. Illustrated by Valerie Littlewood. New York: Greenwillow Press, 1993.

Home Is the Sailor. New York: Viking Press, 1964. London: Macmillan, 1964.

Impunity Jane. New York: Viking Press, 1954. London: Macmillan, 1954.

A Kindle of Kittens. Illustrated by Lynne Byrnes. New York: Viking Press, 1979.

The Kitchen Madonna. New York: Viking Press, 1967.

Listen to the Nightingale. New York: Viking Press, 1992.

Little Plum. Illustrated by Jean Primrose. New York: Viking Press, 1963. London: Macmillan, 1963.

Miss Happiness and Miss Flower. Illustrated by Jean Primrose. New York: Viking Press, 1961.

Mr. McFadden's Hallowe'en. New York: Viking Press, 1975.

Mouse House. Illustrated by Adrienne Adams. New York: Viking, 1957. London: Macmillan, 1958.

The Mousewife. Illustrated by Dana Saintsbury. New York: Viking Press, 1951. London: Macmillan, 1951.

The Old Woman Who Lived in a Vinegar Bottle. Illustrated by Mairi Heddewick. New York: Viking Press, 1972. London: Macmillan, 1972.

Operation Sippacik. New York: Viking Press, 1969. London: Macmillan, 1969.

The Peacock Spring. New York: Viking Press, 1975. London: Macmillan, 1975. New York: Puffin Books, 1986.

The Rocking Horse Secret. Illustrated by Juliet Stanwell Smith. New York: Viking Press. 1977. New York: Viking Press, 1978.

The Story of Holly and Ivy. New York: Viking Press, 1958. London: Macmillan, 1958.
Thursday's Children. New York: Viking Press 1984. New York: Dell, 1984.
The Valiant Chatti-Maker. Illustrated by Jeroo Ray. New York: Viking Press, 1983.

Novels (for Adults)

The Battle of the Villa Fiorita. New York: Viking Press, 1963. London: Macmillan 1963.
Black Narcissus. Boston: Little, Brown, 1939. London: Peter Davies, 1939.
Breakfast with the Nikolides. Boston: Little, Brown, 1942. London: Peter Davies, 1942. New York: Viking Press, 1964.
A Breath of Air. New York: Viking Press, 1951. London: Michael Joseph, 1950.
A Candle for St. Jude. New York: Viking Press, 1948. London: Michael Joseph, 1948.
China Court: The Hours of a Country House. New York: Viking Press, 1961. London: Macmillan, 1961.
Chinese Puzzle. London: Peter Davies, 1936.
Coromandel, Sea Change. New York: William Morrow, 1990. London: Macmillan, 1991.
The Dark Horse. New York: Viking Press, 1981. London: Macmillan, 1981.
An Episode of Sparrows. New York: Viking Press, 1955. London: Macmillan, 1956.
Five for Sorrow; Ten for Joy: A Novel. New York: Viking Press, 1979. London: Macmillan, 1979.
A Fugue in Time. (See *Take Three Tenses.*)
The Greengage Summer. New York: Viking Press, 1958. London: Macmillan, 1958.
Gulbadan: Portrait of a Rose Princess at the Mughal Court. Picture research by Helen Topsfield. New York: Viking Press, 1981.
Gypsy, Gypsy. Boston: Little, Brown, 1940. London: Macmillan, 1940.
In This House of Brede. New York: Viking Press, 1969. London: Macmillan, 1969.
Kingfishers Catch Fire. New York: Viking Press, 1953. London: Macmillan, 1953.
The Lady and the Unicorn. London: Peter Davies, 1938.
The Peacock Spring. New York: Viking Press, 1975. London: Macmillan, 1975. New York: Puffin Books, 1986.
Pippa Passes. New York: Viking Press, 1994.
The River. Boston: Little, Brown, 1946. London: Michael Joseph, 1946.
Take Three Tenses: A Fugue in Time. Boston: Little, Brown, 1945. London: Macmillan, 1987. First published in England as *A Fugue in Time.* London: Michael Joseph, 1945.

Short Stories

Gone: A Thread of Stories. New York: Viking Press, 1968. Published in England as *Swans and Turtles.* London: Macmillan, 1968.
Mercy, Pity, Peace, and Love (with Jon Godden). New York: William Morrow, 1989.
Mooltiki: Stories and Poems from India. New York: Viking Press, 1957. Published in England as *Mooltiki and Other Stories and Poems of India.* London: Macmillan, 1957.

Verse and Verse Translations

The Creatures' Choir. By Carmen Bernos de Gasztold. Translated by Rumer Godden. New York: Viking Press, 1965. Published in England as *The Beasts' Choir.* London: Macmillan, 1965.
In Noah's Ark. New York: Viking Press, 1949. London: Michael Joseph, 1949.
Prayers from the Ark. By Carmen Bernos de Gasztold. Translated by Rumer Godden. New York: Viking Press, 1962. London: Macmillan, 1963.
St. Jerome and the Lion. New York: Viking Press, 1961. London: Macmillan, 1961.

Autobiographies

A House with Four Rooms. London: Macmillan, 1989.
A Time to Dance, No Time to Weep. New York: William Morrow, 1987. London: Macmillan, 1987.
Two under the Indian Sun. By Rumer and Jon Godden. Published jointly in New York by Alfred A. Knopf and Viking Press, 1966. London: Macmillan, 1966.

Other Books

Bengal Journey: A Story of the Part Played by Women in the Province, 1939–1945. London: Longmans, Green, 1945.
Hans Christian Andersen. New York: Alfred A. Knopf, 1955. London: Hutchinson, 1955.
A Letter to the World. By Emily Dickinson. Edited by Rumer Godden. London: Macmillan, 1969.
Mrs. Manders' Cook Book. By Olga S. Manders. Edited by Rumer Godden. New York: Viking Press, 1968.
The Raphael Bible. New York: Viking Press, 1970. London: Macmillan, 1970.
Rungli-Rungliot Means in Paharia, Thus Far and No Further. Boston: Little, Brown, 1946. First published in England as *Rungli-Rungliot.* London: Peter Davies, 1943. A second English edition, published by Macmillan in 1961, is called *Thus Far and No Further.*

Shiva's Pigeons: An Experience of India. Text by Rumer and Jon Godden. Photographs by Stella Snead. New York: Alfred A. Knopf and Viking Press, 1972.

Articles

"Beatrix Potter." *Horn Book Magazine* 42 (August 1966): 391–98.
"A Cool Eye in a Parched Landscape." *New York Times Book Review,* 25 May 1986, 1, 20.
"Do Women Make Good Poets?" *Saturday Review,* 5 January 1952, 7–8, 39.
"Hans Andersen, Writer." *Horn Book Magazine* 66 (September 1990): 554–62.
"An Imaginary Correspondence." *Horn Book Magazine* 39 (August 1963): 369–75.
"Last of the Great Fairytalers." *Saturday Review,* 25 December 1954, 6–8, 32.
"On Words." *Writer,* September 1962, 17–19.
"Opening Speech for Children's Books of the Year Exhibition." *Signal Magazine* 21 (September 1976): 115–17.
"The Poetry in Every Child." *Ladies' Home Journal,* November 1965, 168–70.
"The Secret Garden Revisited." *New York Times Book Review,* 14 May 1961, 36.
"Shining Popocatapetl: Poetry for Children." *Horn Book Magazine* 64 (May 1988): 305–14.
"Tea with Eleanor Farjeon." *Horn Book Magazine* 68 (January 1992): 48–53.
"The Will to Write." *Writer,* May 1985, 13–15.
"Words Make the Book." *Ladies' Home Journal,* January 1964, 32.
"The Writer Must Become as a Child." *Writer,* July 1955, 229. Reprinted from *New York Times Book Review.*
"Writing for Children." *Writer,* July 1977, 18.

Film Adaptations

The Battle of the Villa Fiorita. Warner Brothers, 1965.
Black Narcissus. Universal, 1947.
Breakfast with the Nikolides. Universal films, 1947.
Enchantment. Adapted from *Take Three Tenses.* RKO, 1948.
Innocent Sinners. Adapted from *An Episode of Sparrows.* Rank Organization Film Products, 1957.
In This House of Brede. CBS-TV, 1975.
Kizzy. Adapted from *The Diddakoi* for television.
Loss of Innocence. Adapted from *Greengage Summer.* Columbia, 1961.
The River. Jean Renoir film, United Artists, 1951.
Tottie. Adapted from *The Dolls' House* for television. Kay Webb of Puffin Books.

SECONDARY WORKS

Books

Benstock, Shari. *Feminist Issues in Literary Scholarship*. Bloomington: Indiana University Press, 1987. Includes essays in feminist criticism on themes such as child rearing and the relationship between the domestic and public spheres.

Bettelheim, Bruno. *The Uses of Enchantment: The Meaning and Importance of Fairy Tales*. New York: Vintage Books, 1977. A psychoanalytic interpretation of fairy tales.

Cameron, Eleanor. *The Green and Burning Tree: On the Writing and Enjoyment of Children's Books*. Boston: Little, Brown, 1962. Essays examine the craft of writing for children, with emphasis on the marvelous in children's books. Discusses the importance of place in Godden's work.

Chodorow, Nancy. *The Reproduction of Mothering: Psychoanalysis and the Sociology of Gender*. Berkeley: University of California Press, 1978. Analyzes how women's mothering modes are transmitted and adapted over generations. Discusses the paradox that children expect unity with the mother yet define development in terms of growing away from her.

Egoff, Sheila, ed. *Only Connect*. New York/Toronto: Oxford University Press, 1980. Essays view children's literature as an essential part of the whole realm of literary activity, to be discussed in the same terms and judged by the same standards that apply to any other kind of writing. Views Godden in the context of writers such as Kenneth Grahame, J. R. R. Tolkien, E. B. White, and C. S. Lewis, who did not shy away from difficult themes in children's books.

——. *Thursday's Child: Trends and Patterns in Contemporary Children's Literature*. Chicago: American Library Association, 1987. Following a historical summary of British and American children's literature, examines, by genre, books written in the United States and Britain from 1957 through 1981. Although the author refers to Godden only briefly, chapter 5, "The New Fantasy," presents a useful context for Godden's work.

Eyre, Frank. *British Children's Books of the Twentieth Century*. New York: Dutton, 1973. Discusses publishing developments and their influence on writing for children in the twentieth century; provides an analysis of significant works, including *The Dolls' House;* and attempts to predict which books will become classics.

Gilbert, Sandra, and Susan Gubar. *No Man's Land: The Place of the Woman Writer in the Twentieth Century*. Vol. 1, *The War of the Words*. New Haven: Yale University Press, 1988. Uses Virginia Woolf as a referent for contemporary feminist writers' efforts to revise women's relation to language.

Gilligan, Carol. *In a Different Voice: Psychological Theory and Women's Development.* Cambridge: Harvard University Press, 1982. Records different modes of thinking about relationships and the association of these modes with male and female voices in psychoanalytic and literary texts.

Kuznets, Lois. *When Toys Come Alive: Narratives of Animation, Metamorphosis, and Development.* New Haven: Yale University Press, 1994. Analyzes ways toys come alive in various texts for children and adults, including Godden's doll stories.

Prescott, Orville. *In My Opinion: An Inquiry into the Contemporary Novel.* Indianapolis: Bobbs-Merrill, 1952. Views Godden as one of the modern writers whose work best sheds light on human nature in increasingly decadent times.

Ruddick, Sara. *Maternal Thinking: Toward a Politics of Peace.* Boston: Beacon Press, 1989. Defines maternal thinking and practice as commitment to the preservation, growth, and social acceptability of children.

Rustin, Margaret and Michael. *Narratives of Love and Loss: Studies in Modern Children's Fiction.* London/New York: Verso, 1987. Explores from a psychoanalytic point of view distinctive themes and concerns of postwar British literature. Focusing on the emotional development of children between the ages of five and eleven, discusses how authors create symbolic equivalents of or containers for states of feeling, as exemplified in Godden's doll stories.

Simpson, Hassell. *Rumer Godden.* New York: Twayne Publishers, 1973. The sole previously published full-scale study of Godden's work. Simpson's critique focuses on the novels.

Wintle, Justin, and Emma Fisher. *The Pied Pipers: Interviews with the Influential Creators of Children's Literature.* London: Paddington Press, 1973. Interviews with well-known twentieth-century British and American writers of children's books. Godden discusses her childhood and her approach to writing books for children and adults. The interview highlights Godden's belief that writers should not simplify language in children's books.

Articles

Dukes, Thomas. "Evoking the Significance: The Autobiographies of Rumer Godden." *Women's Studies* 20 (1991): 15–35. Discusses Godden's three autobiographies, viewing their metastory as one of female development. Asserts that the events of Godden's life and her art are so interwoven that it is sometimes difficult to distinguish autobiography from fiction.

Hospital, Janette Turner. "Adventure Was What She Got." *New York Times Book Review,* 3 January 1988, 13. Places Godden in the company of adventurous, capable women such as Isak Dinesen and Beryl Markham and highlights aspects of her biography. Views Godden as a "first-rate story-teller rather than a major literary figure." Criticizes the author's syntax and elitist assumptions.

Moss, Elaine. "Rumer Godden: Prince of Storytellers." *Signal Magazine* 17 (May 1975): 55–60. Discusses apparent oppositions in Godden's life and in her writings for adults and children, concluding that Godden, like India, embraces contradictions. Analyzes stylistic differences in Godden's writing for children and adults.

Tindall, W. Y. "Rumer Godden, Public Symbolist." *English Journal* 41 (March 1952): 115–21. Places Godden in the context of the great symbolist writers of the twentieth century.

Index

The Author

Lynne Rosenthal is associate professor of English at Mercy College (New York). She received her B.A. from the City University of New York and her M.A. and Ph.D. from Columbia University. She has published numerous essays on children's literature and on business and professional writing. She is the director of the American Society for Training and Development's New York City Literacy Project and has chaired several conferences bringing together representatives of the business, professional, and academic worlds to improve writing skills in the workplace.